Austerity

FLORIAN SCHUI

Austerity
The Great Failure

YALE UNIVERSITY PRESS
NEW HAVEN AND LONDON

For information about this and other Yale University Press publications, please contact:

U.S. Office: sales.press@yale.edu   yalebooks.com
Europe Office: sales@yaleup.co.uk   www.yalebooks.co.uk

Set in Janson MT by IDSUK (DataConnection) Ltd
Printed in Great Britain by Gomer Press Ltd, Llandysil, Ceredigion, Wales

Library of Congress Cataloging-in-Publication Data

Schui, Florian, 1973–
Austerity: the great failure/Florian Schui.
   Pages cm
ISBN 978-0-300-20393-6 (cl : alk. paper)
1. Consumption (Economics)—History.   2. Thriftiness—History.
3. Saving and investment—History.   4. Economic policy—
History.   I. Title.
   HC79.C6S263 2014
   339.47—dc23

                                                                2013041994

A catalogue record for this book is available from the British Library.

10 9 8 7 6 5 4 3 2 1
2018 2017 2016 2015 2014

For Cecilia

Contents

Introduction

The austerity policies that have been rolled out in many Western countries have brought all the pain of economic stagnation but hardly any of the promised benefits of debt reduction, renewed growth and prosperity. Nonetheless, support for such measures has remained strong among economists, politicians and substantial parts of the public. How can we explain this steadfastness in the face of economic failure? A way to make sense of this paradox is to place the current debates in historical perspective and look at the deep and ancient roots of arguments for austerity.

For all their topicality, today's controversies over austerity are not new. The notion that individuals, states and societies benefit from limiting their consumption is almost as old as humanity. The term austerity itself goes back to the ancient Greeks, and the question of how much consumption is too much or, indeed, too little was already on the minds of some of the foremost thinkers of antiquity. Since that time, it has remained a focus of political and economic arguments in all ages of Western civilisation, attracting the attention of a rather mixed group of thinkers that included the authors of the Bible, medieval ascetics, enlightened philosophers and modern economists. By reading the current debate as the latest replay of the centuries-old controversy about consumption we can more fully understand the arguments presented by both sides.

Today, the term austerity is often used to denote public spending cuts in general. This captures an important manifestation of austerity policies but it misses their main rationale. Austerity policies are proposed to restore balance in government finances and regain economic dynamism and competitiveness. The former objective is pursued mainly by cutting back on government expenditure that funds individual and collective forms of consumption: for example pensions, health care and education. Where taxes are increased this often leads to a reduction in private incomes and consumption. The second objective, stimulating growth, is mainly sought by lowering the cost of labour, that is, reducing wages and hence individual consumption. Renewed economic dynamism is also expected to result from the reduction of government expenditure and debt: a smaller state is believed to leave more space for private initiative and inspire confidence among private investors and consumers. Austerity policies have many facets but ultimately they are about abstinence from consumption.

Clearly, not all public spending cuts put into place under the label of austerity fall on consumption expenditure. Government spending for investment such as the building of bridges, roads and airports is sometimes reduced, but normally it is protected from cuts or even increased. Expenditure for consumption usually bears the brunt of cuts. This is chiefly because by far the greatest part of government expenditure is for forms of consumption. Any meaningful reduction of government expenditure must therefore mainly reduce these parts of the budget. Moreover, consumption expenditure is also often seen as more dispensable. It is generally accepted that cutting back on infrastructure will damage the prospects of economic recovery and long-term development.

In a similar way, while not all reforms intended to regain economic competitiveness focus on lowering the cost of labour, this is always an essential element. The deregulation of labour markets is mostly geared towards removing laws and institutions that protect workers' and union rights and salaries. Labour usually finds itself in a weaker bargaining position in liberalised labour markets. Falling or stagnating wages are often an important result of deregulation. This makes it possible for companies to produce at a lower cost and become more competitive. The inevitable flip-side of this development is that many wage earners lose income and often have to cut back on consumption.

The current controversy about austerity policies is therefore ultimately about the question of whether or not rewards can be expected for abstaining from consumption. In this sense today's exchanges fit into a centuries-old tradition of consumption critique. Indeed, much of the historical commentary on this topic seems oddly familiar when we read it today. To be sure, much has changed since Aristotle, Aquinas and Voltaire pondered similar questions. Political systems were radically different and so were the ways in which societies and individuals satisfied their material needs: it was as normal for Aristotle that a substantial portion of society – mainly women and slaves – should be excluded from political power as it was for Aquinas that virtually all men and women of his time worked in agriculture and eked out a rather miserable living, without much hope of improvement. And even the much more familiar contexts in which Keynes or Hayek wrote were still different from ours in important respects. Placing the arguments of the past in their own context is therefore crucial to understanding them.

When we review past exchanges about consumption we are bound to encounter unfamiliar vantage points. For the question of how much consumption is right can be approached from many different angles. It is as much a moral, religious or political and even an aesthetic question as it is an economic one. Often the angle from which an author decides to approach the question already predetermines how he or she will answer it.

Today's debates offer a good example of such differences in perspective. The proponents of austerity are often cast as hard-nosed economic experts who advocate unpleasant but necessary measures. The quintessential 'austerian' is the technocrat: the economics professor who turns prime minister in the hour of his country's greatest need, or the experts of the European Commission, the European Central Bank, the International Monetary Fund (IMF), and others who land in a nation's capital to save it from the brink of financial collapse. The considerable power which these experts wield rests primarily on their claim to superior knowledge and understanding of economic matters. Typically they are unelected officials, but large portions of the public support them because they feel safe in the hands of men and women who are well versed in the logic of capitalism and whose vision of the future is not blurred by sentimentalities.

Opponents of austerity, on the other hand, are often perceived as well-meaning but ultimately naive. Many in the public may share their concerns with the social consequences of austerity, but alternative views on austerity, it is often believed, do not sufficiently take into account the inexorable logic of our economic system.

Critical observers have pointed out that reality is often more complicated. The economic performance of countries where austerity measures have been applied most vigorously has often been weaker than in others that were less zealous in reducing public expenditure and reforming the labour market. It is becoming increasingly clear that instead of making the crisis shorter and less severe, austerity has made it longer and deeper than necessary. Critics do not claim that austerity policies will prevent a return of growth for ever. For reasons that are still only partly understood, market economies operate in cycles of upswings and downturns. As a result, periods of renewed growth will also occur with austerity policies in place. The question is, however, whether austerity has led to a downturn that was longer and deeper than necessary and will lead to upturns that are weaker and shorter than they might have been.

The overwhelming evidence that austerity policies do not deliver the desired results has led the IMF to critically rethink its initial analysis. However, this kind of soul-searching has remained the exception. Paradoxically, the failure of austerity to produce any tangible benefits in a reasonable time frame has not led to policy changes. Even where spending cuts have not produced the desired effects of budgetary consolidation and renewed economic growth, political leaders and large parts of the public have stuck to their guns. At first sight this may seem baffling. Weak economic performance should quickly discredit arguments in favour of austerity, and the economic experts who propose them should be the first to acknowledge this. How can we explain this dissonance?

Proponents of austerity are neither fanatics nor less able to understand and judge economic data than others. Instead, the steadfastness with which austerity is defended even in the face of its failure points to a misconception about the case for austerity. Contrary to conventional wisdom, arguments in favour of austerity are not – and never have been – based mainly on economic rationales. Prominent voices have been calling for restraint in public and private expenditure for several thousand years, but if we read their arguments carefully we see that they were rarely concerned with increasing prosperity or with an efficient use of economic resources. The question that is at the heart of modern economics 'How to best satisfy unlimited wants with limited resources?' was not central to these arguments.

Throughout the last 2,500 years those who argued the case for abstinence have based their arguments mainly on moral and political considerations. When the benefits of frugality were first challenged during the European Enlightenment of the seventeenth and eighteenth centuries the critics did not attack the moral condemnations of luxury directly. Instead, they mounted their attack on a different terrain. Excessive consumption may be bad for the soul, they contended, but it makes life more pleasant and prosperous. Their arguments were not about moral judgements at all, but about the question of how economic resources could be used more efficiently to produce greater material comfort.

Since that time, arguments for and against austerity have undergone many permutations but the basic pattern has remained unchanged: proponents of austerity argue on the basis of morality and politics, while their critics use the language of economic efficiency to challenge their viewpoint.

One of the results is that the participants in the great debate about austerity often do not talk to each other, but rather past each other. This form of miscommunication has greatly contributed to making this controversy one of the longest and most inconclusive exchanges in Western culture.

However, the moral nature of pro-austerity arguments has also contributed to the longevity of this controversy in other ways. It may seem surprising that advocacy of a simple lifestyle survived the commercial and industrial revolutions of the eighteenth and nineteenth centuries at all. The modern economic world that emerged from these revolutions is highly dynamic and constantly expanding. Growing consumption drives much of this expansion and nothing seems more out of place in a capitalist society than an austere lifestyle. One might therefore have expected pro-austerity arguments to disappear with the rise of capitalism. And, indeed, they suffered a serious setback when the arguments of the Enlightenment invited the public to celebrate economic growth and stop worrying about moral consequences. But despite these challenges, arguments in favour of limited consumption have proven resilient. Even in today's consumer society the appeal of arguments for austerity has remained unbroken.

In part, this continued appeal is due to a shift in the focus of austerity arguments. For centuries, exhortations to limit expenditure had been targeted at individuals. But modern arguments about austerity focus mostly on collective forms of consumption. Today, only a small fraction of the public condemns the expenditure of private individuals on the latest mobile phone, in the way that writers in antiquity might have condemned excessive expenditure on a finely decorated tunic. On the contrary, there is much public head-scratching about the question of how to boost consumption expenditure by individuals. At the same time, many commentators will warn of dire consequences when individuals pool their resources and – through the state – consume collectively, for example by buying free education or free public transportation. This shift in arguments about abstinence reflects a broader political change in which individualism has eclipsed collectivist political ideas. In part, it was this shift of focus from individual to collective forms of consumption that allowed the message of abstinence to remain compatible with changing economic realities and political ideologies.

However, the persistent appeal of austerity arguments over the last 2,500 years cannot only be explained by their successful adaptation. Indeed, some of their appeal lies in the very fact that they are in some respects outdated. We are children of our time, formed by the reality of a consumer society that praises limitless appetites, but our way of thinking is also shaped by ideas that come from the distant past and that satisfy a deep longing for ethical guidance. Directly or indirectly, most inhabitants of the Western world are imbued with values and ideas that have been formulated long before our time. Even for those who have not read them recently, or at all, the books of the Bible, the writings of Aristotle and even the musings of Aquinas are often part of their cultural and religious formation. When parents tell their children to have only one biscuit instead of the whole packet they impress ancient values of moderation and restraint on them in a way that is more powerful and lasting than even the most assiduous study of classical texts.

The persuasive power of austerity arguments lies in part in the way in which they allude to familiar moral and cultural categories of moderation, sacrifice, selflessness and cathartic cleansing. Even where we do not understand the economic logic associated with austerity arguments – or where they are presented without a compelling economic rationale – their emotional appeal is strong. Austerity speaks to our superego in a way that rational economic arguments never can. Or, in the words of Jonathan Swift: you cannot reason a person out of something they were not reasoned into.

This small book is meant to be a guide to the historical roots of the arguments about austerity in the Western world. It does not offer a comprehensive discussion of the history of economic thought and the focus is only on Western traditions. This limitation reflects the geography of today's austerity policies, which are mostly applied and contested in the industrialised nations of Europe and North America. The main actors and arguments will be introduced along with as much information about their period as is necessary to fully understand what their concerns were. At the same time, we will read the contributions of these men and women – mostly men, really – and their arguments with the question in mind of how their views are linked to today's debates about austerity. The last chapter offers some suggestions of what we may learn from the masters of the past to guide us in our present predicament.

Writing a book of this scope would not have been possible without venturing far beyond the areas where I can claim expert status. Throughout I have relied on excellent research done by others. It is not possible to do justice to all sources that I have used and I will not even try. Notes are only included where direct quotations are used and in order to provide additional commentary to the main text. Some of the authorities that I have used are listed in the bibliography, which is organised by chapter. This, I hope, will compensate to some extent for the lack of more detailed referencing and provide a guide for further reading.

CHAPTER 1

Austere ideas for austere societies
from Aristotle to Aquinas

Although the word 'austerity' derives from the ancient Greek αὐστηρός ('austēros'), Aristotle (348–322 BCE) probably had little use for it. Originally, the term had meant 'dryness of tongue', but in Aristotle's lifetime it was already used to refer to harsh or rough conditions. However, like many of his fellow philosophers, Aristotle led a privileged life. His independent means allowed him to keep his tongue moist with the best that Greece had to offer, including the famed wines of his native Chalcidice in northern Greece. Also in other respects Aristotle was no stranger to the finer things in life: the ancient biographer Diogenes Laertius tells us that 'he was conspicuous by his attire, his rings, and the cut of his hair'.[1]

Aristotle's own comfortable lifestyle hardly seemed to make him a likely voice against excesses of consumption, and yet he raised his voice against them repeatedly. Confusingly, however, he also praised generous expenditure on other occasions. If Aristotle were living today he might well be criticised for inconsistency or for entertaining double standards, but the ambiguities of his views did not raise many eyebrows in his times. His was a fundamentally different society from ours and in order to understand his perspective on luxuries and austerity we first need to get to know the world in which he lived and consumed.

No-growth societies

Aristotle was born in 384 BCE in Stageira, near modern-day Thessaloniki, where his father was the personal physician of the king of Macedon. Young Aristotle received the privileged upbringing that was reserved for the scions of the elite in this period. For the later part of his education he was sent south to Athens, to attend Plato's academy, of which he remained a member for almost two decades. After quitting, he travelled to different parts of the Greek world.

At age 45, Aristotle followed his father's example and entered the services of the Macedonian dynasty: he was called by Philip of Macedon to become the tutor of the king's son, the future Alexander the Great. This employ lasted until 335 BCE, when he returned to Athens and opened his own philosophy school, the famous Lyceum. This second Athenian stay, which lasted for twelve years, was one of his most prolific periods. In these years he wrote the two works in which most of his comments on consumption can be found, the *Nicomachean Ethics* and the *Politics*. He left Athens only after Alexander's death in 323, when he feared that his association with the Macedonian dynasty would make him the target of public anger. However, despite his hurried departure, Aristotle did not become homeless. He retired to a country estate north of Athens which he had inherited from his mother, where he died one year later.

The most salient feature of Aristotle's life was stability. True, he travelled widely, but his itineraries never took him beyond the Greek world. This is also true of his thinking, which always remained essentially ethnocentric. His views on the non-Greek world consistently betrayed a strong sense of superiority. One might object that Aristotle lived through what was arguably one of the most turbulent periods of Greek history. Although comparatively small, the Hellenic world experienced great upheavals. First, during the reign of Philip, the northern kingdom of Macedon became the dominant power in the region, putting an end to Athenian independence. Subsequently, under Alexander, Macedonia expanded to the east by conquering territories in Persia and even further afield. Some of these events directly affected Aristotle, for example when he had to flee Athens after the death of Alexander. In some respects, Aristotle's life may therefore be seen as quite eventful. Certainly he was no ivory tower philosopher.

Nonetheless, in other respects his life and that of many of his contemporaries also exhibited remarkable stability. Most strikingly, there was hardly any change in terms of his social position and economic condition. His father had been the personal physician of a Macedonian ruler and four decades later Aristotle became the tutor of the same monarch's grandson. And while Aristotle, as an outsider, was excluded from political participation in Athens, hardly any restrictions were placed on his economic rights. Even when he had to leave Athens against his will, he did not become destitute. His inherited wealth continued to afford him a privileged lifestyle that was similar to the condition into which he had been born and in which he had lived for most of his life. He died in social and economic circumstances that strongly resembled the ones into which he was born. His legal status remained similarly stable. He was born 'Macedonian' and despite his prestige and the long periods during which he lived in Athens he never acquired citizenship rights there. Nor did he think it strange that legally he remained a foreigner even after decades of residence in the city.

This strong element of continuity was not peculiar to Aristotle's life. Stability characterised the life of most of his contemporaries. However, only a very small number were fortunate enough to remain fixed at a similarly high level. More often, contemporaries were born as small landholders, artisans or slaves and this remained their economic, social and legal condition throughout their lives.

There was much short-term fluctuation in economic welfare as a result of harvest failures. But in the medium and longer term, economies were remarkably stable. Not only did sons mostly embrace the professions of their fathers, but there were also hardly any major changes in the ways that people worked from one generation to the next. This period and much of the Middle Ages were largely devoid of major technological and organisational innovations such as those that drive economic expansion today. Farmers used the same tools and techniques throughout the periods of Greek and Roman dominance, and much of Europe still used the primitive Roman plough well into the Middle Ages. Manufacturing employed only a fraction of ancient populations and here, too, innovation was rare and the traditional ways in which artisans worked, as well as the products they made, were subject to very little change. None of the innovations that revolutionised economic life in later periods and that generated the ability to produce vastly more with the same amount of human labour occurred in the ancient world.

Socio-economic stability was a hallmark of individual lives and consequently of contemporary societies as a whole. In the same way as most men died with a fortune roughly comparable to the one they were born with, so most societies did not become significantly richer or poorer over a generation or even over longer periods. The only exception to this may be the Roman Republic, but its increase in prosperity was mainly due to the plundering of occupied territories and had little to do with home-made economic growth.

The exact levels of contemporary economic growth are unknown, but the existing estimates are sufficiently accurate to give a sense of the order of magnitude. Today, most economic historians think that economic growth in the ancient world ranged on average from 0.05 to 0.1 per cent per year. Such increases are minuscule compared to the levels of growth that are considered normal in the modern world. Moreover, we need to remember that the level of economic output was low in the first place. The goods and services represented by 1 per cent of growth in a pre-industrial society were only a tiny fraction of what 1 per cent of growth means in terms of additional wealth and use values in today's advanced economies.

When we look at the social and economic development of ancient societies we find a near complete lack of economic growth and of social mobility. In other words, in Aristotle's day people knew from experience that the size of the pie changed as little as the size of the share that was assigned to them. It is in light of this reality – radically different from ours – that we need to read Aristotle's seemingly contradictory comments on consumption and abstinence.

Of necessities

In many respects Aristotle was truly a 'worldly philosopher'. He had a clear opinion on the political questions of the day and his writings display a genuine curiosity about all aspects of life. Therefore, when he enquired into the question of how humans might attain happiness it was perfectly clear to him that this was not only about putting aside enough time for leisure and the cultivation of friendships, but that there was also a more prosaic dimension to this question. 'Neither life itself,' he pointed out in the *Politics*, 'nor the good life is possible without a certain minimum supply of the necessities.'[2] Much of his thinking on ethics then centred on the question of balance. In his *Politics*, but even more extensively in his *Ethics*, Aristotle discussed the question of how much that 'minimum supply' of material goods was that allowed men to live the 'good life'. Material excess, as much as material want, was likely to prevent men from attaining this ideal state. This view is hardly surprising given the central position that the notion of the 'golden mean' occupied in classical philosophy. All classical Greek philosophers, including those of the often misrepresented Epicurean tradition, rejected hedonism and advocated a measured approach to consumption and pleasure.[3]

Temperance was therefore one of the principal virtues described in the *Ethics*. In book III, Aristotle explains that temperance was mainly about avoiding excessive bodily pleasures, specifically the 'touch and taste' sensations caused by the consumption of physical objects.[4] Pleasures of the mind such as 'love of honour' or the 'love of learning' belonged to a different category, as did the more fleeting sensations of enjoyment caused by 'objects of vision' or 'hearing'.[5] The notion of temperance applied to pleasure that was caused by what we might term 'consumer goods': physical objects that were owned by the consumer and at least to some extent used up in the process of enjoyment.

Aristotle is most concerned about the pleasures of eating and the excesses of those he calls 'belly-gods'.[6] However, while he is clear that over-indulgence is 'culpable', Aristotle is tantalisingly imprecise about how much is too much. Being a man of the world he did not fail to acknowledge that a certain amount of physical wants – including those of the 'bed' – were natural and should be satisfied. But on the whole, Aristotle advised, 'the appetitive element should live according to reason'.[7] The reader who is looking for practical advice on acceptable levels of consumption in this part of the *Ethics* is bound to remain frustrated by the philosopher's vagueness.

More specific answers can be found in book IV of the *Ethics*, where Aristotle turns to the 'virtues concerned with money'.[8] For Aristotle, the appropriate level of expenditure was not merely a matter of balancing accounts. His judgement depended crucially on what was bought by whom and for what purpose. No matter whether an individual was contributing to the welfare of the community in a very substantial way by paying for a 'trireme' – a state-of-the-art contemporary warship – or in a smaller way by contributing to an official mission to an oracle or religious game, or whether he was simply furnishing his house or throwing a wedding party, the same maxim applied: 'we [should] have regard to the agent as well [as to the expenditure] and ask who he is and what means he has; for the expenditure should be worthy of his means, and suit not only the result but also the producer.'[9]

Aristotle's answer to the question of how much expenditure was right was thus a resounding 'it all depends'. Most importantly, it depended on the means and status of the individual in question. 'Right expenditure' resulted when object and extent of expenditure were in harmony with the social rank and the wealth of the man footing the bill and of those enjoying the benefits of his expenditure.[10] In practice, Aristotle's recommendations meant that everyone was to consume according to their place in society. In his eyes, the austerity of a rich and respected man would have been as deplorable as an excessive level of ornamentation in the house or on the dress of a humbler man. This way of looking at consumption may be contrary to our notions of equality and equity, but it was typical of the highly hierarchical societies of the ancient and medieval worlds. The underlying spirit is captured well in the Roman phrase 'quod licet iovi, non licet bovi' ('Gods may do what cattle may not') that was also used as a proverb in medieval times.

As with spending, Aristotle also made an important distinction between different ways of making money. Here, too, it was crucial for him that economic behaviour remained attuned to the natural order of society. Indeed, our term 'making money' would hardly have satisfied Aristotle, whose ideal was that of a man who spent out of the wealth he rightly owned, trying to use it wisely, but not trying to increase it. Just as he frowned upon spending above one's station, trying to earn more than one was due was suspect.

Aristotle distinguished between natural and unnatural ways of acquiring goods. The most natural way of acquiring goods was to extract them directly from nature. Farming, hunting, mining and other means of harvesting the bounties of nature were acceptable methods of satisfying material needs. This is hardly surprising, given that this was the manner in which the vast majority of contemporaries went about securing their livelihood. Barter was also permitted, but only as long as the objective was not to increase one's wealth but to reduce waste by exchanging goods that one possessed in excess for others that one lacked. Where the objective of exchange was to increase one's wealth it became trade, which Aristotle condemned as unnatural and reprehensible. As with consumption, the concern was to avoid economic behaviour that was not in harmony with traditional social structures.

Aristotle's main question was different from that on the minds of many people today. He was not concerned with increasing prosperity. Rather he contemplated the question of how to make good use of whatever amount of wealth one was entitled to by tradition and heritage. Perhaps betraying his privileged upbringing, he wrote in his advice to the wise household manager: 'Wealth should be at hand from the start.'[11] To ask how the wealth of an individual or of society as a whole could be increased was an 'unnatural' question for Aristotle.

Should we then dismiss Aristotle's arguments as cynical? Was he merely attempting to add a veneer of moral respectability to a social and economic status quo that was above all beneficial to members of the upper classes like him? He wanted and advocated a system that kept him and his peers in place. There is clearly a conservative element in Aristotle's outlook: in traditional societies, like those of ancient Greece, individuals who consumed more or less than they were supposed to were a threat to stability. Low growth rates meant that there was not much additional wealth generated each year. Anyone who hoped to expand their consumption, that is have a richer lifestyle and possessions, could only do so by taking resources from someone else. Today one person's pay rise is not necessarily linked to another person taking a cut. However, if productivity increases are minuscule, as they were in ancient

Greece, then the economy is largely a zero sum game. In such a static context, moderation of appetites was not only good moral advice, it was crucial for the functioning of the social and political system.

Aristotle did not consider whether or not the hierarchies and institutions of his time ought to be accepted or contested, or whether they were just or unjust. For him, the fundamental structures that were at the root of the social order of his time were given by nature: man was by nature a 'political animal' (i.e. an inhabitant of a Greek polis), the state was an institution given by nature, and nature also made humanity in pairs of unequals such as 'master and slave' or 'husband and wife'. He saw the order in which he lived as a natural one. Consequently, the task set before mankind could not be to question the natural order, but to understand it and live in harmony with it.

It would be ungenerous to criticise Aristotle for failing to foresee the possibility of radical change in the ways in which humans organised their interaction. Our knowledge of history warns us against thinking of our own world as 'natural' or immutable. But Aristotle did not witness or know about the kind of revolutionary changes which turned European societies on their heads in later centuries. Today we know that our world is the product of a long chain of social, economic and political revolts. And many still find it hard not to think of themselves as living at the end of history.

However, Aristotle's perspective on consumption and abstinence is not only the result of his conservative outlook. It also reflects a specific notion of virtue. When we ask 'what is the right thing to do?' many today will consider the question without paying much attention to who is taking the action. If we try to answer that question in a utilitarian fashion, we will say the right thing to do is that which will bring about the greatest happiness for the greatest number. In this view, only the result matters and the person and the motives behind the act become unimportant. This is the way in which nineteenth-century thinkers such as Jeremy Bentham or John Stuart Mill would have answered this question.

Others, like the eighteenth-century philosopher Immanuel Kant, took a different view. For Kant a virtuous act was one that was in accordance with his supreme maxim, the categorical imperative: 'I ought never to act, except in such a way that I can also will that my maxim should become a universal law.'[12] In other words, only if we can confidently face the question 'what if everyone did that?' are we acting in a morally acceptable way. The question is thus whether or not we are fulfilling our duty to consider the welfare of mankind in our acts. Neither for the British utilitarians nor for Kant does it matter who carries out the act and what that person's condition and feelings are.

This was radically different from Aristotle. For him, it was not enough that the right thing was done. It also needed to be done by a good person who was happy to act in this way. An individual who needs to force himself or herself to act in the right way can therefore not act virtuously. Seen in this light, it may easily happen that two people who are doing the same thing are, from a moral point of view, acting in very different ways. Similarly, two people consuming the same amount or spending the same sum may be seen to be doing different things. Aristotle was thus not so much applying double standards as looking at the question of moral conduct in a more holistic way than we often do.

However, what is perhaps most important for our argument is that all of Aristotle's considerations about the right level of consumption and abstinence centred on moral and political questions. Purely economic mechanisms hardly played any role in his reasoning. Nowhere does he examine what the consequences of changes in the level of consumption of one person would be for that of other individuals. Neither does he ask whether a change in consumption habits would lead to prosperity or austerity for society as a whole. Or how a more efficient use of resources might allow an increased level of consumption. Instead, what he was interested in were the consequences of consumption for the individual's chances to achieve happiness and lead the 'good life'. Equally important to him was how patterns of consumption might or might not be in harmony with social and political structures ordained by nature. But economic questions in the way in which we would understand them today were not on his mind when he argued for moderation in matters of consumption.

Christianity

Besides Aristotle and other ancient philosophers the most important source for the message of austerity in Western culture is without question the Christian tradition. In contrast to the case of Aristotle, no one is likely to point to incoherence between the message and the messenger's way of life. Jesus not only preached restraint in matters of consumption but, as far as we know, also lived a live of exemplary simplicity.

In many respects, the world that Jesus inhabited resembled that of Aristotle. Certainly, European geopolitics had changed dramatically. Rome had risen to imperial glory and erstwhile powerful dynasties and cities of Greece had been relegated to the rank of provincial powers. Sophisticated Romans were aware of the enormous debt they owed to Greek culture, but the centre of political and military power had clearly shifted to the western Mediterranean. In Jesus's time the city of Rome dominated an empire that stretched from the English Channel to North Africa and from the Iberian Peninsula to the valley of the Jordan river. Important technological and military changes had taken place compared to Aristotle's time. The invention of cement, improvements in mining techniques and the development of superior military technology all contributed to Rome's rise.

In other respects not much had changed. Roman society was as static and stratified as that of Greece. As in Greece, much of the economic and social life of the Roman Empire was organised around the institution of slavery. Slaves could become freemen and it was possible to move through the ranks of society in other ways, but by and large there was not much scope for individuals to change their social condition. At times, able and ruthless military leaders spectacularly rose to the highest political positions. But mostly, the rights and privileges that Romans and inhabitants of imperial provinces enjoyed at the end of their lives resembled closely those they had been born with and, indeed, those of their parents and grandparents.

The same was true of income and wealth. Economic growth remained gradual at best throughout the Roman period. The innovations in construction and mining contributed to higher productivity, but they remained isolated and were not complemented by progress in other areas. This is not to say that luxuries did not exist or did not play an important role in Roman culture. Even today, visitors to archaeological sites are struck by the splendour and sophistication of many Roman dwellings. Jewellery and artwork produced at the time rival many of today's luxury products and the excesses of contemporary elites in the consumption of food and drink remain legendary. But such lifestyles were the preserve of a comparatively small and closed-off section of society and remained far removed from what ordinary men and women could reasonably aspire to.

The eye of the needle

If we read Christ's message of restraint and altruism against the backdrop of this social reality, it sounds almost revolutionary. In the Sermon on the Mount and elsewhere the founder of Christianity was unequivocal in his condemnation of material excesses. Leading a life concentrated on material consumption, he told his assembled followers, was against God's will. 'No one can serve two masters,' he warned, 'you cannot serve God and wealth.'[13] The accumulation of wealth on earth was an obstacle to 'storing up wealth in heaven'.[14]

Concerns with consumption were bound to detract from important spiritual growth: 'Do not worry, saying, "What will we eat?" or "What will we drink?" or "What will we wear?"'[15] Ideally, for followers of Christ such material concerns were to become secondary. As long as they strove 'first for the kingdom of God', material matters would fall into place.[16] From a Christian perspective, questions of material welfare paled in significance compared to spiritual welfare. It was man's calling to live a virtuous life and use the transitory period of earthly existence to prepare for eternal afterlife.

In this respect Jesus's message was a continuation of older Jewish traditions: the story of Sodom and Gomorrah in the

Book of Genesis is one of the most impressive stories about human sin and divine punishment in Western culture. The story is often read as a warning of the consequences of sexual depravity but, as the theologian Stephen Long points out, the sins committed in the two cities were 'more to do with economics than with homosexuality'.[17]

In the Old Testament, the inhabitants of Sodom and Gomorrah were denounced for their self-absorbed greed and their obsession with material possessions. The prophet Ezekiel called them 'arrogant, overfed and unconcerned', and according to Jewish traditions greed led the Sodomites to outrageous cruelty.[18] In particular, they invented perfidious ways to avoid charitable giving: nominally, Sodomites followed the obligation of assisting the poor, but when they gave to beggars they inscribed the donor's name on the coins and ingots which they gave. Subsequently, the Sodomites refused to sell food to recipients of their gifts. The beggars starved and the 'charitable offerings' were reclaimed by the donors. This mockery of social justice was a flagrant breach of the covenant with God. The inhabitants of Sodom and Gomorrah had broken man's promise to God to create a humane society governed by brotherly love and solidarity. Consequently, God turned away from them. Hence in the older Christian and Jewish traditions, gluttony and selfishness were clearly seen as contrary to a good and God-pleasing life.

Even those of us who did not grow up in an explicitly Christian cultural context are bound to sympathise with this message of restraint. Who would not agree with Jesus's word that there is more to life than food and more to the body than clothes? Nonetheless, it is important that the biblical perspective on wealth and consumption differs fundamentally from the way in which the question is often approached today. Nowhere is this clearer than in Jesus's famous admonition that 'it is easier for a camel to go through the eye of a needle than for someone who is rich to enter the kingdom of God'.[19] An excessive concern with wealth is negative partly because it violates the covenant with God that is based on the promise of creating a humane society on earth, but also because it prevents access to a blessed afterlife. With the possible exception of very confident atheists, this message continues to resonate with many people today. Even if we are not certain about what the afterlife has in store for us, or whether there is such a thing, we still grew up in a culture that was founded at least in part on a deep-seated suspicion of prosperity. Politicians who suggest that we may have to contend with a period of austerity can therefore be certain of finding audiences who sympathise with their message without necessarily engaging with the associated economic rationales.

Compared to Aristotle's concern this marks a shift in perspective. Aristotle asked whether certain forms of consumption would get in the way of individuals leading the 'good life'. This was clearly an ethical way of framing the question, but it was also a decidedly 'this worldly' perspective. In the Christian understanding, consumption matters because it can be an obstacle to a virtuous life on earth, but it matters also because it may form an obstacle to entering paradise. Despite this difference, there is an important common ground between the two perspectives: both were entirely unconcerned with the way in which economic interaction worked. The effects of luxurious or austere lifestyles on the number of people employed, the amount of goods produced, the level of prices and similar mechanisms were simply not considered.

Despite some common traits, the Christian perspective on wealth and consumption differed from Aristotle's viewpoint in one important respect. Whereas the Greek philosopher called for a level of consumption that was in accordance with social rank and individual circumstances, the Christian position knew no similar differentiation. Wealth was an even greater obstacle to going to heaven for a member of the social elite than for a poor peasant or a slave. In practice, the latter categories were only rarely exposed to the temptations of excessive consumption, and there is a socially conservative component of early Christianity in that the austere lifestyles which most contemporaries led willy-nilly were declared to be virtuous. However, while preaching poverty to the poor may be seen as a way to administer an opiate to alleviate the pain felt by the impoverished majority, preaching poverty to the rich had a potentially explosive effect. This was one of the reasons why the interpretation of the often radical statements of the Sermon on the Mount – such as the call to ignore material questions altogether – was at the centre of theological debate throughout the centuries.

Asceticism

The medieval Scholastic Thomas Aquinas (1225–74) argued that not all the teachings of Jesus applied to all the faithful in the same measure. Some counsels – among them poverty and chastity – only applied to those seeking perfection, mainly 'professional Christians' such as nuns, monks and priests. Ordinary believers, striving for mere salvation rather than perfection, could content themselves with less ambitious standards. In particular, a life in poverty was not required of them. This became and remained the official position of the Catholic Church, but the tension between social reality and the Christian message was felt strongly at the time.

One of the most important reactions to the self-restraining aspects of the Christian message was the formation of ascetic religious movements from the fourth century onwards. The newly emerging religious orders emphasised abstinence as the way to true Christianity and aimed to distinguish themselves from other parts of the Church that were increasingly preoccupied with worldly power and wealth. One of the most radical exponents of this current, Francis of Assisi (1182–1226) decided to renounce the wealth and privilege into which he was born as the son of a successful merchant in order to follow the example of Christ and live a life in poverty. Even the angry reaction of his father, who treated his son to regular beatings, could not change Francis's mind. Besides the personal disappointment which the father may have felt, his violent reaction likely reflected the fear of the socially corrosive power that lay in Francis's decision. If the wealthy and privileged themselves stopped believing in wealth and privilege what – or, rather, who – was to stop the social order from collapsing? Social systems are usually well equipped to deal with opposition from below, but nothing is more likely to strike fear into a social elite than a feeling of sinking morale among its own.

Other Christian thinkers have found different ways to deal with the tension between Christ's teachings and a social reality of economic inequality. Sixteenth-century reformers such as Martin Luther argued that the teachings applied merely to the realm of the spiritual. Where worldly affairs were concerned, worldly laws and norms applied. In other words, the spiritual commitment to poverty did not translate into a challenge to the property rights of the rich in the temporal world.

Ancient philosophers and the religious tradition of Christianity both found ways to accommodate historical realities in which luxury spending and ostentation played an important role. Still, both persuasively argued that for most people an austere lifestyle was the right path to take. Disciples of Aristotle who wanted to lead the 'good life' on earth and Christians who wanted to follow the principles of their faith on earth and hoped for salvation in the afterlife were well advised to tame their appetites. Most striking for a modern reader is the way in which these arguments were constructed. Much consideration was given to the welfare of the soul during this life and after death, individual happiness, and a harmonious coexistence in society.

Other issues, more familiar to us, were completely ignored: when Aristotle counselled for a limitation of expenditure for the equipment of warships, he did not worry what his advice would do to the business prospects of Athenian shipyards. Neither is there any consideration given in the Bible to the point that the lavish spending of the inhabitants of Sodom and Gomorrah probably made high-end manufacturing thrive in the two cities.

This kind of prioritisation of moral over economic considerations may seem only rational if an apocalyptic firestorm is understood to be a possible sanction for unethical conduct. But even where the stakes were not quite as high, economic questions, in the way that we understand them, were not part of the contemporary approach to gauging the right level of individual consumption. In part, the more limited importance of economic questions was simply the result of the fact that contemporaries were faced with a world in which 'the economy' did not exist as a distinct sphere that obeyed its own logic and laws and therefore required its own set of explanations. Also, the development of contemporary economies rarely deviated from familiar trajectories. The unforeseen events and radical transformations of economic life that stimulated much of the economic thought of later generations were largely absent in this age. It is therefore hardly surprising that contemporaries did not care more about the economic mechanisms associated with consumption.

Although economies have fundamentally changed since those times, the teachings from those distant epochs have remained enormously influential. Today most people in the West grow up in a world that is radically different from that of Aristotle or Jesus, but their teachings continue to be part of our 'cultural hard-wiring'. Fewer and fewer inhabitants of the Western world read the Bible or are practising Christians, and the number of those familiar with the works of Aristotle is even smaller. But when we are asked to respond to moral questions of right and wrong we often cite arguments from the classic works of Western culture, without knowing it.

This matters for our attitudes towards consumption. In our daily life we may not pay much attention to the message of moderation, but as a part of our upbringing we know that we should. Therefore arguments about tightening our belts and ending excessive spending fall on fertile cultural ground. As a part of our cultural heritage, we tend to have a moral affinity with the message of austerity. We bring this cultural bias to all discussions of the topic, no matter how much they seem to revolve around economics. John Maynard Keynes famously observed that 'practical men, who believe themselves to be quite exempt from any intellectual influence, are usually the slaves of some defunct economist'.[20] True as this is, participants in economic debates and even professional economists are just as much slaves of centuries-old moral and religious teachings.

CHAPTER 2

Austerity v. reason
from Mandeville to Voltaire

In the end, the lure of material pleasures proved to be stronger than the warnings of pagan philosophers and Christian preachers. From the late Middle Ages, traditional feudal societies declined in Europe and most historians agree that a widespread fascination with a rapidly expanding material culture played an important role in this transformation. In different ways, contemporaries tried to become part of the new world of commerce and consumption and leave behind them the austere lifestyles of their ancestors.

In this period the first intellectuals broke with the centuries-old tradition of condemning excessive consumption – called 'luxury' by contemporaries – as a moral evil. Many thinkers of the seventeenth and eighteenth centuries were fascinated by the capacity of commerce – driven by unbridled consumption – to bring prosperity and comfort to previously austere societies. They challenged the validity of some of the moral and religious arguments that had been put forward by critics of consumption. But more importantly, they started to look at the question of consumption from an economic rather than from a moral point of view. This chapter is dedicated to these first 'economistic' attacks on the idea of austerity. Bernard

Mandeville (1670–1733) and Voltaire (1694–1778) were among the earliest and wittiest writers to challenge the ideological status quo. We will read their spirited attacks along with the replies of Jean-Jacques Rousseau (1712–78) and others who refused to be convinced by the new prophets of plenty.

Consumer revolutions

When the Enlightenment writers of the seventeenth and eighteenth centuries began to popularise new perspectives on consumption, fatal damage had already been done to traditional feudal societies. The unstoppable rise of commercial society had started to transform the lives of many Europeans, in particular urban dwellers. As ancient and medieval thinkers had predicted, moderation had been crucial to maintaining the social status quo. When new patterns of consumption emerged, the foundations of feudal society began to crumble. The lure of consumption contributed to the rise of a new order which contemporaries called commercial society.

Initially, the transformation was slow and affected mainly the rich and powerful. The discovery of new shipping routes meant that long-distance trade in exotic spices and precious commodities like silk and porcelain expanded slowly but steadily. Increasingly, these luxuries became part of the public displays of power of traditional elites. When the French and English kings met in 1520 in the north of France they put on such an extraordinarily sumptuous display of luxuries that the location later came to be known as the Field of the Cloth of Gold.

In Renaissance Italy, rival dynasties tried to outdo each other by staging ever more lavish state dinners featuring ever greater amounts of exotic ingredients. Perhaps the most impressive display of this 'culinary arms race' was staged by the duke of Ferrara who, in 1529, threw a magnificent dinner for the wedding of his son to a daughter of the king of France. During the eight weeks of celebrations enormous amounts of precious textiles and tableware were used. But even more striking were the amounts of food consumed and the ingredients used. The menu included the latest in contemporary kitchen trends, including boned capon (a cockerel castrated to make it grow fatter) covered with sugar, more capon with a sauce made of sugar, pepper, cinnamon, ginger, cloves and saffron, as well as sausages sprinkled with sugar and cinnamon. There was also eel with sugar and cinnamon.

These examples cannot do justice to the variety of dishes offered but they point to a common characteristic: the indiscriminate and generous use of sugar and exotic spices in all types of dishes. The expensive condiments were liberally applied to everything from vegetables to meat, fish and desserts. In this way, food was turned into an edible manifestation of taste, power and wealth. To us, many of the dishes may seem rather unappetising. However, we should remember that Renaissance men and women would probably be equally unimpressed by the kind of food that is used for the purpose of social distinction today: the lean, sugar-free, organic fare consumed by today's elites would not have cut the mustard at any princely banquet in early modern Europe.

The cost of procuring edible and other luxuries put an enormous strain on the budgets of even the wealthiest contemporaries and anyone trying to imitate their lifestyles. For some, the oceanic expansion of European powers also led to the discovery of new sources of revenue. Spanish and

Portuguese aristocrats who were able to tap into the influx of gold and silver from South America could expand their luxury consumption with greater ease. However, many other aristocrats across Europe were hard-pressed for revenue and the credit offered by newly enriched merchant princes only offered temporary relief. Consequently, the desire to consume more and more refined wares led many members of the feudal elites to explore new sources of revenue.

In particular, they needed to increase cash revenues in order to purchase exotic luxuries. The agricultural and homespun products which they received as part of feudal dues from serfs and vassals could hardly match the appeal of the wares procured by long-distance commerce. Therefore, lords were keen to substitute rent payments for feudal obligations or use their land themselves to produce easily marketable crops. Another way to satisfy the new need for specie was to grant additional freedoms to the increasingly self-confident and prosperous towns of medieval Europe. In return for greater independence or additional trade privileges, urban dwellers paid new taxes or indemnified the feudal lord with one-off payments. Adam Smith later noted that in this period many landlords sold their birthrights for a handful of 'trinkets and baubles, fitter to be the playthings of children than the serious pursuits of men'.[1]

Feudal society was undermined not only by the childlike tastes of many aristocrats, but also by changing consumer habits among the lower ranks of society. Improving trade routes and economies of scale led to a drop in the prices of imported luxuries such as coffee, tea, sugar and tobacco. Goods that had been the preserve of privileged members of society were now increasingly within the reach of ordinary people.

At the same time, European manufacturing began to offer appealing local alternatives to imported luxury products. In particular, domestically made cotton goods and other textiles became more attractive and were affordable for a greater part of society. At least initially, this transformation was not driven by mechanisation. Until the late eighteenth century, the availability of cheaper consumer goods was mainly made possible by the invention or adaption of new materials and by new ways of organising production that took advantage of economies of scale and the division of labour.

The new, more widely available consumer items confronted common men and women with some of the same problems that the rich had faced earlier: would-be consumers needed cash to replace homespun wares with more attractive ones that could be bought on the markets. The result was an 'industrious revolution': more people worked longer hours, and more frequently they worked for a wage rather than within their household. A shift away from traditional forms of mostly agrarian production to a more modern, commercial economy was the result. As a harbinger of the 'industrial revolution', a revolution in consumer habits undermined the political and economic foundations of medieval societies: the personal loyalties on which the feudal system had been built were increasingly replaced with relations of commercial exchange.

Worldly poets

Perhaps unsurprisingly the rapid development of a consumer culture also led to new ways of thinking about austerity. The teachings of the ancients and the Christian tradition that had dominated views about consumption for centuries were increasingly questioned. Although the changes in consumer habits were palpable almost everywhere in urban Europe, it still took a great deal of courage openly to challenge the prevailing ideology of abstinence. When, in 1705, Bernard Mandeville pointed to some of the contradictions between moral ideals and economic reality in his famous poem *The Fable of the Bees*, his work caused outrage. It was investigated by a grand jury that pronounced it a 'nuisance' and contemporary commentators referred to him as 'man devil'.[2] And when Voltaire published his poetic defence of luxury in 1736, he could avoid arrest only by fleeing to the Netherlands.

Both authors were well acquainted with the pleasures of consumption. Mandeville, a native of the commercially advanced Netherlands, had settled in the equally prosperous city of London. There he embraced a successful career as a physician and occasional author. Not much is known about the circumstances of his life, but his lifestyle most likely included all the comforts that were available to members of his class in a metropolis such as London: coffee, tea, sugar, tobacco, imported spirits, wines and fine clothes. This was even more true of his contemporary Voltaire, who grew up in Paris. The city was then, as now, Europe's luxury capital. From an early age Voltaire was fascinated with the 'trinkets and baubles' that were on offer in the city. One of his first poems was an ode to a beautifully decorated tobacco box that had been confiscated by one of his teachers and which he missed dearly. This fascination with luxury stayed with him all his life.

In addition to being a gifted writer, Voltaire was also a shrewd businessman. His talents gave him the means to indulge in everything which Paris had to offer at the time. Perturbed by his son's choice to eschew a career in the law in favour of becoming a writer, Voltaire's father stipulated in his will that his son should only come into his inheritance on his thirty-fifth birthday if he had by then embarked on a 'well ordered career', that is, if he had renounced his plans to become a professional poet. However, at age 35 Voltaire had already made a fortune of his own and was able to enjoy a luxurious lifestyle without any help from his family. The fourteen rooms of the house which he later inhabited in Paris with his lover Émilie du Châtelet (the French translator of Mandeville's *Fable of the Bees*), were filled with everything which the city's suppliers of luxury had on offer: porcelain, silverware, damask-covered chairs, lacquered furniture (following the latest Chinese fashion) and paintings, including one entitled *Venus Scourging Love*.

Clearly, both men knew how to make and spend money. But they were also educated men and knew that many of the pleasures in which they and many of their peers indulged were condemned by a powerful coalition of classical philosophers and religious authorities. In particular, the views of the latter were not merely of theoretical importance: when Voltaire moved to Geneva in the 1750s he ran into trouble with local authorities when he added gold decorations to the interiors of his house and began to stage private theatrical performances. This kind of luxurious indulgence was not well regarded in the Calvinist city and Voltaire was eventually forced to desist from his plans. Voltaire, Mandeville and others took to writing apologias for luxury because, in different forms, the tensions between economic reality and moral dogma were part of everyday life for many contemporaries.

Interestingly, Manderille and Voltaire did not challenge the prevailing morality directly. No attempt was made to declare that luxury consumption was morally innocuous or even virtuous. The challenge was mounted in more indirect, but no less powerful ways. First of all they questioned the moral authority of those who preached frugality but often led a luxurious life themselves. Mandeville ridiculed the Roman philosopher Seneca who liked to 'swagger about … contempt for riches'. Sarcastically, Mandeville offered to write 'twice as much about poverty as ever he did, for the tenth part of his estate'.[3] He could quite easily have mounted a similar – if not entirely fair – attack on Aristotle. The religious authorities of his day do not fare much better at the hands of Mandeville. Priests, monks and nuns preached 'austerity' and 'contempt for riches', but in practice they were often more devoted to 'gluttony, drunkenness and impurities of a more execrable kind than adultery itself'.[4]

Voltaire ridiculed the hypocrisy of well-fed churchmen preaching simplicity in a similar manner. In his poem *The Man of the World*, written in the late 1730s, Voltaire imagined an encounter at the dinner table with a prelate who openly admitted that he wished to see the poet roast in hell as a punishment for his writings in defence of luxury. But while the 'rank bigot' was relishing the prospect of Voltaire's future torments, he was also filling himself with wine from the Canary Islands and coffee from Arabia served on precious porcelain and silverware. Denouncing the hypocrisy, Voltaire wrote:

> For thee the world at work has been,
> That thou at ease might vent thy spleen
> Against that world, which for thy pleasure
> Has quite exhausted all its treasure.
> Thou real worldling, learn to know
> Thyself, and some indulgence show

To others, whom so much you blame
For vices, whilst you have the same.[5]

Even in his apology for luxury Voltaire, like Mandeville, continued to write about 'vices' when talking about the enjoyment of luxuries. While he did not suggest that they were anything other than vices, he believed that they had become so common that it was time for some generous tolerance towards them.

The wages of sin

However, the main blow to the case for consumer abstinence was dealt by another set of arguments. The alternative title of Mandeville's poem sums them up in the shortest possible way: 'private vices, publick benefits'. Vices they may be, harming man's prospects of being saved in the afterlife or of leading an Aristotelian 'good life' on earth, but they also brought great benefits to society. The principal public benefit of the private vice of excessive consumption was the unprecedented prosperity that commerce had brought to many places across Europe.

The bees in Mandeville's story resembled the inhabitants of his native Rotterdam, or any of the other great commercial hubs of Europe. Like many urbanites today, they were busy building their careers, trying to outsmart others, sometimes bending the law to their advantage and generally trying to get as much material gain out of life as possible. There are lawyer-bees who 'kept off hearings wilfully, to finger the refreshing fee' and physician-bees who much 'valued fame and wealth, above the drooping patient's health'.[6] No more self-absorbed

beings could be imagined than Mandeville's bees. But, aston-
ishingly, rather than producing chaos and mayhem, the result
of every bee behaving at its worst was a beehive that lived in
'luxury and ease'. How was this possible?

> Luxury employed a million of the poor,
> And odious pride a million more.
> Envy itself and vanity,
> Were ministers of industry;
> Their darling folly, fickleness,
> In diet, furniture and dress
> That strange ridiculous vice, was made
> The very wheel that turned the trade.[7]

Despite the immoral motives, expenditure for consumption
had a benign effect. Millions of workers found employment
and lived better than the rich had lived before society was
gripped by luxury and vanity. Just how beneficial private vices
were to the society of bees became abundantly clear when, in
a sudden turn of events, the bees became virtuous. Vanity
disappeared and expenditure on anything but the necessary
dried up. Customers became frugal and, in a scenario bending
the limits of the imaginable, merchants turned honest.
Mandeville invited his readers to witness the consequences
and see for themselves 'how honesty and trade agree'. In the
reformed hive the 'building trade is quite destroyed' while
'artificers are not employed'.[8] Those who had previously found
work in the luxury trades were deprived of their livelihoods
and had no money anymore to spend even on necessary things.
The bee economy was now firmly set on a downward spiral
and the insects eventually relocated from their once thriving

hive to a hollow tree in order to continue their existence as poor but virtuous insects.

Which was better: living an immoral but prosperous life or claiming the moral high ground and living in austerity? Voltaire had no doubts. He dismissed the charms of earnest simplicity that reigned in the Garden of Eden and concluded his defence of luxury with a homage to the place that in his time most resembled Mandeville's wicked but splendid hive: 'Paris to me's a paradise.'[9]

In Mandeville's fable, the sinful pursuit of self-interest and unfettered spending led not only to prosperity, but also had another benign effect. Everyone was only pursuing their own interest, and yet, this led to 'parties directly opposite assist[ing] each other as if it were for spite'. This miraculous effect did not quite happen all by itself. Vice needed to be 'lopped and bound' by good laws.[10] But if a wise government channelled and guided the passions of its citizens, rather than trying to repress them, then the pursuit of self-interest led to peaceful collaboration and served the interest of all.

Mandeville's story about a society that was prosperous and stable without having virtue dealt a devastating blow to those who contended that austerity was the price to be paid for a good life in general and for social stability in particular. Most contemporaries agreed with Voltaire that they would much rather live comfortably in Paris than primitively in the Garden of Eden. Of course, the success of these new ideas did not only come from Mandeville's and Voltaire's elegant verses. As Victor Hugo later pointed out, nothing is more powerful than an idea whose time has come. Without any doubt, the time of commerce and consumption had now come in a powerful way in many parts of Europe. The arguments against abstinence were supported by the daily experience of millions of Europeans, many of whom lived in cities that thrived economically because of a rapidly expanding consumer culture. Nor was this development limited to the great commercial hubs. Around the middle of the eighteenth century, new companies trading in exotic luxury goods sprang up in places as peripheral as East Frisia, and more established trading companies multiplied their profits.

Many contemporaries no longer cared about the immorality of the consumption of 'superfluities' such as coffee, tea and sugar. Indeed, they did not think of them as superfluities anymore. As living standards began to rise, consumers started to react angrily when they were prevented from indulging in forms of consumption which had been considered immoral not so long before. Where monopolies and customs duties limited access to commodities that were now seen as necessities, smuggling, unrest and open revolt could be the consequences. The Boston Tea Party was a case in point: one reason that the tea monopoly of the East India Company was much resented at the time was because of associated questions of taxation. But the monopoly was also attacked because it was a way in which government prevented local consumers from freely choosing where to buy their supply of the fashionable beverage. In Europe the history of the eighteenth century is littered with similar instances where far-reaching political conflict was triggered by governmental interference with newly formed consumer habits.

Everywhere, old ideas about the virtues of frugality were swept away on a wave of cheap wares and clever new arguments. The change in the economic and intellectual climate was so radical that proponents of abstinence struggled to formulate a convincing response. Their arguments looked tired and old-fashioned. It almost seemed as if no one took them sufficiently seriously anymore to even bother with a direct response. The economic arguments of the apologists for consumption simply drowned out the moral concerns of the other side.

The frugal Jean-Jacques

Even the most gifted critic of consumerism of the eighteenth century, Jean-Jacques Rousseau, could not change this. Rousseau was perhaps a more credible critic of consumerism than most. He was a native of frugal Geneva, the city that had denied Voltaire his gold ornaments. Rousseau opposed the mannerisms of fashion because of deeply held convictions, but in many periods of his life he was also quite simply forced into a frugal lifestyle by lack of money. He left Geneva and his family at an early age and made ends meet by working as a tutor, secretary and servant. However, Rousseau also associated himself with wealthy benefactors on several occasions. Their generosity afforded him the opportunity to move in elite circles in Paris, Venice and London. Yet, he never truly embraced the lifestyle of the elegant and well-heeled and always seemed more comfortable as a lonely wanderer than in the company of urban worldlings.

It was therefore perhaps no surprise that Rousseau made his breakthrough as a writer with a tract that was a radical attack on the consumer society of his time. In 1749, he noticed an advertisement in a newspaper that publicised an essay competition held by the Academy of Dijon. Participants were asked to answer the question of whether the development of arts and sciences had contributed to refining the moral character of man.

In the language of the day, the term 'arts' had a much broader meaning than today. It did not merely refer to the fine arts but also to the productive arts, including most forms of manufacturing and commercial activity. In his memoirs, Rousseau later recollected that he became a different man upon seeing the advertisement. A whole new way of looking at civilisation opened up to him at that moment. Whether or not Rousseau's account of the event was later embellished is impossible to know, but there can be no doubt that when Rousseau stumbled upon the advertisement it was a momentous instant in the history of political thought. In response to the academy's question, Rousseau wrote a short tract entitled *Discourse on the Moral Effect of the Arts and Sciences*, which promptly won first prize. The prize, but even more the radical content of the small book, immediately catapulted Rousseau into the literary limelight.

The writings of Mandeville, Voltaire and others had made it fashionable in intellectual circles to endorse the blessings of commercial society. Rousseau disagreed. To him, the increase in material comforts came at a high price. He conceded that under the auspices of commercial society, commerce and political stability were mutually reinforcing. However, another consequence was that economic success and appearances became the chief preoccupation of individuals. All other emotions, drives and desires were subordinated to these ends: no one would allow personal animosity to get in the way of a lucrative business deal and no true feeling of friendship was required to extend an invitation to a dinner party if the potential guest could add glamour to the event. Such patterns of behaviour helped to control the passions that could disrupt social life and went a long way to greasing the wheels of commerce. But as a result men lived dishonest, corrupted lives.

They no longer acted in accordance with their feelings and their personalities, but lived for others and through others. Individuals were completely alienated from their true selves by the tyranny of consumption. Moreover, under these circumstances the state could never be more than an oppressive institution. In a society where private wealth was the highest aim and greed was the all-pervading motivation, it became the main role of the state to protect the security of private property. Given the unequal distribution of wealth, this meant that the state would forever be an oppressive agent protecting the wealthy minority against the impoverished multitude.

Upon reading Rousseau's pamphlet, Voltaire complained that it was an invitation to regress to a primitive past and begin crawling on all fours again. But was it really? In *The Social Contract* Rousseau later explained how he imagined a future society. Living like a noble savage was not part of this utopia. But a limitation on the appetite for consumption and a greater amount of equality would almost inevitably be necessary if his political vision of a truly free and democratic society was to become reality.

Rousseau's arguments resonate with readers today as much as at any time over the past 250 years and his views have shaped the ideas of social reformers ever since. But their contemporary impact remained limited because they suffered from the same shortcoming that made many other arguments in favour of abstinence irrelevant to the way in which most people lived and thought at the time: Rousseau's criticism focused once again on the moral and political consequences of consumption. As such, his views exercised a powerful influence, but he had no reply to the persuasive economic arguments of Mandeville and his school of thought.

Examining the question of consumption from a new vantage point was the main contribution of authors like Mandeville and also the secret of their success. They shifted the debate about consumption to a terrain where it was almost impossible for the proponents of abstinence to win. Rather than asking how people *should* behave economically they asked how individuals *will* behave and what effects they produce by behaving in a certain manner. Once the question was reframed in this way the answer no longer depended on ethical norms but rather on a careful analysis of the inner logic of commercial society. Inevitably, such an approach led to the conclusion that expanding consumer demand was necessary for prosperity and stability in a commercial society. The arguments of early theorists of capitalism may have been presented in the form of tales about beehives and the Garden of Eden, but underneath they provided penetrating economic analysis. Above all, they persuasively explained the inexorable logic that linked consumption to economic progress and prosperity. Such arguments based on rational analysis and economic facts appealed to an enlightened public that was increasingly doubtful of the religious teachings that underpinned the glorification of austerity.

Perhaps the most important analytical insight which Mandeville and others brought to the debate about consumption was their understanding that commercial economies relied on dynamic and interconnected processes. In particular, they understood that one man's expenditure was another man's income. Therefore, if expenditure decreased, the same happened to income. This distinguished commercial economies from traditional ones and, even more importantly, it distinguished economies from private households. It was perfectly possible for a private household to limit expenditure while keeping its income stable or increasing it. But the same was not true of a system composed of many households and businesses that provided each other with employment and income. Mandeville's favourite bête noire was therefore the common notion that 'National frugality enriches a country in the same manner as that which is less general increases the estates of private families'.[11] A clear understanding of what modern economists call 'feedback loops' distinguished Mandeville from many proponents of austerity in the eighteenth century and later periods.

So decisive was the blow dealt to arguments favouring consumer abstinence in the eighteenth century that they lost much of their prominence in public debates. Instead, the notion that in matters of consumption more is almost always preferable to less became one of the fundamental assumptions of modern economic reasoning. Today, there is general agreement that growing consumption is a precondition for economic growth and the satisfaction of potentially unlimited material wants is accepted as one of the principal objectives of economic activity.

Arguments in favour of limiting private consumption have continued to exist in various guises and we will return to them later in this book. However, since the time of the commercial revolution such arguments have been the preserve of reformers and revolutionaries who wanted to defeat capitalism in one way or another. Like the authors writing in ancient and feudal times, those who later wanted to overcome the system often questioned the benefits of expanding individual consumption. However, those who embraced capitalism and its inner logic lost interest in the alleged benefits of consumer abstinence.

CHAPTER 3

Austerity for capitalism
from Smith to Weber

'Frugality fatigue' became a major cultural and economic phenomenon in eighteenth-century Europe. But the notion that abstaining from consumption had its merits did not disappear completely. It soon made a comeback in a different guise. As economic thinkers further dissected the newly emerging market economy they noticed that there was another vital ingredient for its expansion. Besides a strong appetite from consumers, the system also needed significant amounts of capital. Most of the dramatic increase in production that could be witnessed since the late eighteenth century was made possible by more efficient ways of organising production and by the use of powerful machines: if, at the end of the eighteenth century, one man could make 4,800 pins in a day rather than one, that was the effect of the division of labour. And if, around the same time, one worker could simultaneously spin yarn on 120 spools instead of one, this was due to the invention of a new machine, the spinning jenny.

One crucial ingredient made both the division of labour and the introduction of new machinery possible: capital. The division of labour could only be set in motion with sufficient funds to equip a factory and buy a stock of raw materials. Initially, this required comparatively small amounts of capital. However, from the early nineteenth century, when large-scale mechanisation and the use of fossil fuel became the norm in many branches of industry, enormous and increasing amounts of capital were required for further growth. Capital truly was the 'lever of riches' that had the power to multiply the productive capacity of human labour in a way that was unprecedented in human history.

But where did capital come from? Surely if everyone always spent all their income on 'trinkets and baubles' in a Mandevillean way, no money would ever be put into things so entirely devoid of glamour as a pin factory or a spinning jenny. Clearly, what was required were individuals who abstained from consumption in the present in order to make savings and subsequent investments possible. Thinkers of Mandeville's generation did not worry much about this question because the amounts of capital used at the time were still very limited. But during the nineteenth century and after, some of the brightest minds in economics have argued over the question of who made the sacrifices that paved the way for the unparalleled economic take-off and what had triggered this wave of abstinence.

These questions were not merely of antiquarian interest. Capital had another important characteristic besides multiplying the productivity of labour. The owners of capital were entitled to a share of the output that was produced with the help of their assets. But while the profits of capital owners could reach dizzying heights in the nineteenth century, the other group that laid claim to a share of output, workers, often lived at or below the breadline. The question of where capital originated from was therefore not merely academic. The story that economists told about the origins of capital had far-reaching implications for the legitimacy of the competing claims that workers and capitalists made to the fruits of labour.

Two rival stories dominated the nineteenth century. There was a rosy one, in which virtuous and far-sighted individuals decided to renounce the lure of consumption, invested their wealth and were subsequently rewarded for their sacrifice by handsome profits. The other story, much less reassuring, involved peasants, workers and slaves who were forced to further reduce already low levels of consumption. This made their lives miserable and short, but allowed others to take a greater share of production and accumulate the necessary funds for profitable investments. Most prominently, Adam Smith (1723–90) and Max Weber (1864–1920) introduced their readers to a world in which a select few, in possession of virtue and economic reason, adopted austere ways of life and were amply rewarded later. In contrast, Karl Marx (1818–83) and Thorstein Veblen (1857–1929) conjured up a world in which there was nothing virtuous or rational about abstinence. Above all, in their view, the people doing the abstaining and those reaping the benefits were members of different groups: for Marx and Veblen the term 'exploitation' best described the processes associated with the accumulation of capital. Defying the chronological order, this chapter discusses the rosy views of Smith and Weber before presenting the critique of Marx and Veblen.

Austerity and accumulation

Smith observed that his contemporaries normally parted with their monies with one of two distinct purposes in mind: either they spent them for 'present enjoyment' or for 'future profit'.[1] The poor and the very rich were mostly in the former category. The poor because their incomes were so low that they needed to immediately convert them into food, drink, clothing, housing and heating if they did not want to perish. The very rich acted in a similar way because they found it near impossible to renounce any of the comforts they were used to. Those born to great wealth, Smith observed, tended to be more concerned with 'elegance of … dress', 'equipage' and 'household furniture'. 'Ornament' was more important to such men than 'profit'.[2]

It was left to those occupying the socio-economic middle ground, often living in circumstances not too different from Smith's own, to forgo 'present enjoyment' for 'future profit'. As a professor of moral philosophy and tutor and later as a tax official, Smith had a comfortable income. He could afford more than the necessities of life: a pleasant home, neat dress and some of the luxuries of his time such as tobacco, tea and sugar. There were numerous items on Smith's shopping list from which he could abstain without going hungry or suffering unbearable living conditions.

Unlike the poor, the middle classes had a choice about how to use their income, or at least parts of it. And unlike the very rich, the middling sort often possessed a good measure of business acumen. Not many understood economic matters as fully as Smith, but an extraordinary eagerness for material gain and a keen, almost instinctive grasp of how money could be made by investing it could be found among the men and women growing up in this environment more often than elsewhere in society. In addition, successful business undertakings were a mark of distinction for members of the middle class rather than a stigmatising experience, as they were still seen by some of the more traditional members of the contemporary nobility.

If business-savvy members of the middle class decided to renounce 'present enjoyment' in favour of 'future profit' this could have far-reaching consequences for their own economic conditions but also for society as a whole. A nation that could boast many such individuals was bound to become vastly more prosperous. Holding back funds from consumption and investing them in a productive business turned mere wealth into capital, which made the division of labour and other labour-saving innovations possible. Capital could multiply the productivity of human labour by several orders of magnitude. The volume of goods produced every year and hence the wealth of the nation and everyone's ability to consume useful and beautiful products grew rapidly thanks to the sacrifices of those individuals who had previously abstained from consumption.

Capital also changed the ways in which different categories of individuals interacted with each other. In a long-gone era that Smith called the 'original state of things', capital and private ownership of land did not exist. Under such conditions 'the whole produce of labour belonged to the labourer'. The worker had neither 'landlord nor master to share with him'.[3] But since this golden age had passed and most production involved the combination of capital owned by one individual with the labour power of another person, the product of labour had to be shared. Since the owner of capital 'lent' his accumulated stock – fruit of his earlier abstinence – to the worker, he could expect a share of the output in return. Smith called the share of the owner 'profit' and that of the worker 'wage'.

Was it fair that the capitalist should receive a share without lifting a finger? Smith was not much concerned with this problem. After all, the labourer's ability to produce vastly more was the result of his use of capital. Also, it was not by chance that the capitalist found himself in the comfortable position of receiving an income without working. This was the reward for his earlier abstinence from instant gratification. In this view, profit was a reward for those endowed with sufficient economic understanding to see the potential of investments and enough strength of character to resist the lure of the instant gratification that could be found in consumption. While praising the resulting benefits to society, Smith remained suspicious of the selfish motives that guided individual entrepreneurs. He was, without using these terms, much more an admirer of capitalism than of capitalists.

However, for later economic writers who built on his analysis, abstinence came to be closely linked to heroic entrepreneurial figures who had proven their intellectual and moral superiority and who were rewarded for this by leading their businesses and whole nations to greatness and prosperity. Alfred Marshall (1842–1924), the leading economist of his time, saw saving as closely associated with a morally superior concern for the welfare of future generations. To many who thought like Marshall, capitalists were not simply rich people who lived in a society where their wealth continued to make them richer. There was a degree of merit built into the economic arrangements of the day. This gave legitimacy to the way in which society worked and also seemed to offer an opportunity for anyone who emulated thriftiness and learned business sense to join the ranks of the economic elite.

Austerity and the Protestant ethic

Smith never spent much time worrying about the question of what equipped certain individuals with the fortitude to resist the lure of consumption. He clearly did not think poor people and scions of 'old money' to be very capable of it, but besides this he did not venture any guess as to why some individuals emerged in this way while others did not. It is quite possible that he did not have any views on this question. For him, the central question was how capital was accumulated and it certainly mattered *that it was accumulated*, but whether one person or another carried out this task was ultimately secondary from an economic point of view.

It was perhaps for this reason that it was not Smith, the founding father of modern economics, but Max Weber, the founder of sociology, who formulated the most influential thesis on the question of what predestined men to become capitalists. Like Smith in eighteenth-century Scotland, so Weber was a towering intellectual figure in early twentieth-century Germany. Among the most prominent of his texts was the essay in which he addressed the cultural preconditions for the development of capitalists and capitalism. The thesis that Weber proposed in his essay *The Protestant Ethic and the Spirit of Capitalism* in 1905, and that has remained influential under the label of the 'Weber thesis', was as simple as it was bold: early entrepreneurs were able to accumulate capital because they led austere lives and they did so because this was God's will, or at least that was what they took it to be.

Weber was inspired to examine links between economic behaviour and religious convictions when he noticed that the Protestant territories in the recently unified German empire outperformed the Catholic areas in economic matters. He may also have been intrigued by the different character traits he could observe in his parents. His father, largely irreligious and born to considerable wealth, was a man who enjoyed earthly pleasures, while his mother, of Calvinist descent and persuasion, was a model of a more frugal lifestyle. The different attitudes led to considerable tensions in the family, which may have contributed to Weber's falling out with his father.

Weber argued that the precepts of Protestantism were better suited to bringing about patterns of behaviour that were necessary for a successful capitalist society, or, for that matter, to be successful in capitalist society. In particular, Weber viewed 'asceticism' in private life and a deep devotion to professional success as qualities that were more readily found among Protestants than elsewhere in Christianity. Because these were also qualities that enabled would-be entrepreneurs to accumulate capital and invest it successfully, Weber saw 'elective affinities' between Protestantism and capitalism.

According to Weber, it was not the teachings of Calvin in their original form, but rather bastardised popular versions that helped to build the foundations of capitalism.[4] Much of the argument hinges on different views held by Protestants and Catholics on predestination. While all Christians believe that salvation is ultimately God's gift and that no amount of pious works or God-pleasing conduct can alter the course of events, emphasis differs. Catholic observances such as confession and absolution and the medieval trade with indulgences led Luther, Calvin and others to protest because these practices seemed to imply that God's decisions could be swayed by man's actions. Instead, reformers insisted that salvation was exclusively God's doing and that men only found out about their fate on the Day of Judgment.

God's will could not be changed, and neither could God's will for a person's salvation be known. To cynics this could have been an invitation to lead a merry and unconcerned earthly existence. However, devout followers of Calvin did not see it in this light. For them, God's commandments were to be followed not because benefits could be expected but simply because they were God's will. Prominent among the things that God expected from men, at least in Calvin's interpretation of Jesus's teachings, was to lead a simple life and fully devote themselves to their professional calling. Whether or not the faithful succeeded was ultimately without importance for their salvation, but since it was God's will they were still called upon to try as hard as they could: clad in frugal black the prosperous citizens of Calvin's Geneva accumulated rich savings, which they invested in watch manufacturing and other trades that they pursued with the divinely ordained discipline. This would probably have been enough to give the city an edge over other urban centres with differently minded populations.

Similar patterns of behaviour were reinforced by the spread of new popular beliefs that were at odds with Calvin's teachings, but nonetheless extremely helpful for the smooth functioning of capitalism. Many of the faithful found it difficult to accept Calvin's view that God's plans could not be known before Doomsday. Confronted with the probing questions of their flocks some Protestant preachers therefore began to deviate from Calvin's dogmatic views. While changing God's will remained impossible, they conceded that the faithful might look for 'outward signs' that signalled that they enjoyed God's grace. Success during earthly existence, in particular prosperity, could be seen as such a sign of approval. Unsurprisingly, economic success became one of the primary preoccupations of many Calvinists. This was despite the fact that the additional prosperity could not be converted into added comfort or luxuries to any significant extent because frugality remained an absolute imperative. However, being seen as chosen gave individuals considerable prestige among their religious peers. Lots of hard work, investments that turned good profits and no spending on 'trinkets and baubles' meant that exponential growth of capital accumulation was the happy result of the adoption of Protestant ethics.

Abstinence thus made an astonishing comeback in economic thought. Mandeville had branded miserly abstinence from consumption a danger to prosperity. But as Smith and Weber pointed out, abstinence did have a place in capitalism because it was the precondition for investment. This nexus became a cornerstone of economic analysis. But there was also a moral dimension to their understanding. In their accounts, austerity was about choice. Individuals were not forced into abstinence. They chose this way of life because they followed moral and religious precepts and they were able to stay the course. They had sufficient strength of character to renounce instant gratification in favour of future benefits in the shape of profits, or salvation, or both. The fact that those who collected profits on their investment had previously distinguished themselves in this way added to the moral legitimacy of profits. Anyone in the nineteenth century, and after, who asked the potentially explosive question of why already wealthy capitalists should earn substantial profits while workers often lived in poverty could find solace in reading Smith and Weber. Capitalists, the classic writers reassured their readers, were the 'deserving rich'.

Austerity for the masses, capital for the elites

Not everyone found Smith's story compelling. In particular, one very careful reader begged to differ and wrote a formidable rebuttal. Karl Marx devoted an entire chapter of *Capital* to quashing what he considered starry-eyed accounts of early accumulation. For him, it was violent coercion rather than virtuous choices that led to the first accumulations of capital. Or, in his own words: 'capital comes [into the world] dripping from head to foot, from every pore, with blood and dirt.'[5]

Marx agreed with Smith that only abstinence from consumption could make possible the accumulation of capital and hence productive investments. But they disagreed when it came to the question of who had done the abstaining. For Smith and Weber, frugality and business acumen were twin qualities and individuals who possessed both were the heroes of early capitalism. Here Marx forcefully disagreed. Certainly, abstinence from consumption had occurred on a massive scale. But it was neither voluntary nor undertaken by the elites. Instead, the economically and politically powerful forced the already poor majority to lower their consumption even further and then pocketed the difference: austerity was for the masses, accumulation for the few. The rise of capitalism was therefore not an edifying exercise in self-restraint, but a brutal process driven by 'conquest', 'enslavement', 'robbery' and 'murder'.[6]

Marx devotes much of the chapter to supporting his claims with examples, mostly from English history. Most prominently he discusses the enclosure movement of the eighteenth century and related transformations in which landlords stopped renting their land to peasants and put an end to its communal use. Instead, vast areas were enclosed and used for grazing sheep for wool production. The peasants who had previously sustained themselves by working the land lost their incomes as a result, but landowners made good profits and could accumulate substantial capital for investment. In a similar way, guild regulations and acts of parliament were used from the end of the fifteenth century to lower the wages of jouneymen and apprentices. The resulting higher profits enabled guild masters and other manufacturers to save and invest more.

Marx also pointed to the large fortunes made in the colonial slave trade and invested in manufacturing ventures in Britain and elsewhere in Europe. Much of the accumulation of wealth by merchants in port cities such as Liverpool was made possible by barring thousands of slaves from even the most basic forms of consumption. It was therefore, as far as Marx was concerned, not the virtue of capitalists, Protestant or not, but the misery of millions of peasants, manufacturing workers and slaves that provided the 'seed money' of capitalism.

There was an important flip-side to this process of 'forced saving'. While the wealthy and powerful grew even more wealthy and powerful, the mass of the population was deprived of land, tools and other property. Stripped of these assets it became impossible for them to produce anything on their own. Henceforth, production was only possible if the labour power of proletarians, without land or property, was combined with the tools and raw materials of the capitalists. Proletarians, in Marx's famous words, were 'free in a double sense': free to sell their labour power, but also free of other commodities to sell and free of the capital goods necessary for autonomous production.[7] Consequently, they were not only free to work for a capitalist but also obliged to do so if they did not want to starve. In this way, early accumulation produced not only capitalists but also their social counterpart: proletarians.

Marx never bothered to explain what led feudal lords, who had been exploiting their serfs for centuries, to switch gears and fully expropriate them. In Weber's story the Reformation triggered a change in behaviour in future capitalists and led them to become more frugal and business-minded. In Marx's analysis it is much less clear what triggered the change. Marx would probably have pointed to the increasing demand for wool and other commodities that arose from the development of manufacturing, but he did not give much thought to the origins of this development.

In his comments on early accumulation, John Maynard Keynes (1883–1946) later offered a monetary explanation: the influx of vast amounts of gold and silver from Latin America led to increased demand for luxury goods that were often made or procured by manufacturers and merchants in northern Europe. Increased demand together with legal limitations on wage increases led to profit inflation. The promise of high profits functioned as a stimulus to increases in raw material supplies and investment in manufacturing and commercial enterprises. For Keynes it was stolen gold, not Protestant piety, that triggered the shift in economic behaviour in early modern Europe.

Although Marx would have none of Smith's story of capitalism founded on the frugality of capitalists, he was willing to concede that early entrepreneurs had made an important contribution. They had acquired their wealth by unsavoury means, but they still deserved credit for turning these funds into capital. Unlike earlier expropriators, they did not hoard the money or spend it on building pretty but unproductive chateaus. They invested it in pin factories, textile mills and trade companies. They caused untold suffering, but they were also responsible for helping humanity on to a new stage of development. Marx wanted to overcome this stage as quickly as possible, but nonetheless he saw it as a new, higher, and necessary phase on the way to Communism.

The predatory charm of the bourgeoisie

Soon after Marx's death, another economist began to chip away at whatever was left of the classic narrative about the thrifty and heroic founders of capitalism. Thorstein Veblen was a merciless critic of capitalism and his comments on capitalists were even more caustic than Marx's. Unlike Marx, who was the son of a comfortably off lawyer, Veblen was not only ideologically but also culturally an outsider to bourgeois society. His parents had emigrated to the United States from Norway and he grew up on the family farm in western Wisconsin. His superior intellect earned him a Yale PhD and several appointments at the best American universities. But despite becoming a famed author and intellectual, he always found it difficult to be accepted by his academic peers. Suffering discrimination on account of his social origins and his agnosticism, he refused to blend in with bourgeois society. Along with middle-class manners – he cared little for his appearance and was notoriously untidy – he rejected the narrative that economic elites were telling about themselves and their origins. Marx had attacked the notion that the thrift of capitalists was behind original accumulation, but he had still credited them with a useful function within the system. Veblen, in contrast, saw the Rockefellers, Guggenheims and Carnegies of his time as self-obsessed and vain predators whose money grabbing did not serve any purpose but the financing of an obscenely ostentatious lifestyle.

In his *Theory of the Leisure Class* of 1899 Veblen coined the term 'conspicuous consumption' for what he saw as the main activity of elites throughout history: leaving the toil of productive labour to the masses, the powerful used their predatory prowess to separate workers from the fruits of their labour. At times, these transfers were hidden behind more or less complex social arrangements, but mostly it was simply a matter of taking. According to Veblen, there was no economic rationale behind this process: elites take just because they can.

Contrary to the view of classical economists like Smith and Marx, elites did not give anything back to society by fulfilling an economic function. Veblen's elites did not spend their days at the helm of companies, steering them through the adversities of economic reality. Rather, they whiled away their time in enormous mansions in Newport, in the ballrooms of the Waldorf Astoria, and in the grand hotels of Europe. For him, the purpose of the accumulation of wealth, if there was one at all, was to continually re-enact cultural and social superiority. Through conspicuous consumption and an ostentatious display of their leisure, the elites distinguished themselves from the rest of society and tickled the desire of the masses to emulate them. In Veblen's view, this was crucial to keeping the system stable: blinded by the stunning displays of wealth, the lower orders busied themselves with futile attempts to climb socially rather than to overthrow the existing order.

In some respects Veblen's was almost a Mandevillean vision of the economy. For him, consumption, not production, was the key to understanding social and economic interaction. But how did he account for investments in a world that seemed to revolve exclusively around consumption? In Veblen's time, growing concentration led to the formation of large trusts that were increasingly managed by a class of engineers and professional executives. Veblen put his faith in this new class of professionals. For him the figure of the entrepreneur was rapidly becoming obsolete. Technocrats took investment decisions and the necessary funds were provided by a financial sector that was run in a similarly anonymous manner. Moreover, in ever more prosperous societies nobody – neither elites nor masses – needed to abstain from basic consumption in order to make investment possible. Savings were more abundant and banks, stock exchanges and other financial institutions now efficiently matched savers and investors across national economies and often also internationally. Decades of rapid economic growth and technical innovation meant that the primary challenge for businesses had shifted away from finding sufficient funds for investment. Now the difficulty was to find profitable investment opportunities and markets in which to sell additional production.

Who was right?

If we look back at this controversial debate that lasted for over a century and included some of the greatest minds in the history of economics, we are left wondering – who was right in the end? Should we accept Smith's and Weber's view in which freely chosen, perhaps divinely ordained austerity laid the foundations of economic progress? Or was the reality closer to a Marxian and Veblenesque scenario in which brutal exploitation laid the foundation for more veiled and institutionalised forms of exploitation?

When Keynes reviewed these exchanges in the late 1920s he pointed to the fact that it might well be impossible to answer such questions conclusively because of the lack of reliable economic data. Nonetheless, he expressed doubts that the voluntary abstinence of entrepreneurs had played an important role in stimulating economic growth in the past. His doubts were primarily based on a theoretical argument: in history, individual decisions about saving were disconnected from economic needs for investment; individual decisions about thrift were unlikely to produce resources for investment when and where they were needed. Moreover, he argued, the amounts of wealth accumulated by voluntary saving were far too small to supply the substantial investments necessary for economic development in many stages of history.

The work of modern historians supports Keynes's doubts. The enclosure movement is today widely seen as closely linked to early industrial development. Modern research has also shed light on the important role that fortunes from the slave trade and piracy played in the early stages of the industrialisation of Europe. A close connection existed between such forms of 'forced saving' and subsequent investments in domestic manufacturing.

While there is much historical evidence about the violent side of early accumulation, it is much more difficult to substantiate the importance of voluntary saving. In particular, attempts to find empirical evidence to support Weber's thesis have revealed many difficulties. Recently, the economic historian Davide Cantoni attempted the Herculean task of testing the Weber thesis but found no conclusive evidence to support it. Clearly, it is difficult to test such a complex thesis as Weber's empirically and the last word in this matter has certainly not yet been spoken. Nonetheless, the available historical facts suggest that individuals who chose an austere way of life were a culturally important phenomenon in the early stages of industrialisation, but not one that can on its own explain the economic dynamics of this period. Forms of voluntary saving certainly played a role, but they were accompanied by much involuntary abstinence. Both phenomena ultimately fulfilled the same important economic function in the early stages of industrialisation, but only one could provide the material from which a moral tale about the origins of modern economic life could be crafted.

CHAPTER 4

Austerity for stability
from the Great War to the next

By the first half of the twentieth century abstinence was no longer mainly a question of individual behaviour. Instead, whole societies collectively adopted austerity as a means to restore monetary and financial stability. After the First World War, many European governments cut their expenditure to return to balanced budgets and deployed deflationary policies to control inflation and restart economic growth. Reduced government expenditure, unemployment and falling wages led to often painful reductions in collective and individual consumption. Timing and circumstances differed, but ultimately the austerity policies of the interwar period were motivated by a common desire to leave behind the post-war turmoil and return to greater stability.

Four years of extraordinarily brutal and costly warfare had thrown the European continent into the greatest disorder it had seen since the French Revolution. However, the economic consequences of the war were only fully felt once it had ended. Among the most visible signs of the continent's precarious situation were runaway inflation and enormous public debt. Regaining financial and monetary stability therefore became a priority of governments. But their quest was about much more than balanced budgets and stable prices: in the collective imagination the financial and monetary stability of pre-war Europe was associated with a golden era of prosperity, social and political stability and, indeed, moral rectitude. The ethical, even spiritual dimension was unmistakable.

This period was also characterised by a political struggle over the question of whether the way forward for European countries was a restoration of the pre-war status quo or whether it was time to embrace progressive social ideas. Universal male suffrage had become a reality in most of Europe by this time. The left believed that not only politics but also society and economy should be organised in a more democratic manner. However, conservatively minded contemporaries were convinced that a return to the blessed age of the pre-war era was only possible through a process of economic and moral atonement. It was inevitable that societies and states should undergo programmes of austerity designed to correct the excesses, moral and economic, to which the war had led. Although these debates were primarily about financial and monetary questions, the arguments put forward often comflated the economic and the moral. In many instances, moral categories and political calculations were ultimately more influential than economic reasoning and financial facts. The moral and political imagination of contemporaries played a central role in many interwar debates about economic policy. Two cases are particularly salient: Britain's brief but calamitous return to the gold standard from 1925 to 1931, and Germany's even more ill-fated attempt to respond to the 1929 financial crisis with a programme of austerity.

Return to a higher standard

Like most other European countries, Britain had left the gold standard in the context of the war. Before that, the value of the pound was fixed in terms of a certain amount of gold. Since most other currencies were also pegged to gold in the pre-war period, the gold standard guaranteed stability of international exchange values. With some variations this monetary system had been in place since the nineteenth century and was often hailed as one of the pillars of European peace and prosperity. However, along with many other certainties on which the societies of nineteenth-century Europe had rested, the gold standard became a victim of the Great War.

Britain and the principal countries involved in the conflict needed enormous amounts of credit to pay for the cost of armaments. However, the amount of currency that central banks could issue under the gold standard was limited by the requirement that banknotes be convertible at face value into gold on demand. To ensure convertibility legal regulations often fixed the ratio of currency in circulation in proportion to the gold reserves held at the central banks. Absent a miraculous addition to the gold reserves of the central banks, the required amounts of credit could only be made possible by issuing additional currency over and above the level possible under the gold standard.

This problem was made worse by the rapid increase in prices during the war. Inflation almost inevitably follows on the heels of war, but this nexus was particularly strong in the case of the First World War. It was the first industrial war of this scale and the industrial age wrote the rules of this conflict.

Individual bravery and military genius hardly mattered anymore in this conflict. It was a war of attrition, and the mobilisation and destruction of economic resources played a crucial role in the balance of power. Historians often pay much attention to the more innovative pieces of military technology that were deployed in this conflict. But planes, tanks and poison gas were ultimately not nearly as important as the ability to produce vast amounts of more conventional pieces of military equipment such as guns, cannon, helmets and bayonets, or, even more banally, the procurement and distribution of food and clothing for soldiers.

In the early twentieth century, the economies of Europe were better able to produce this military equipment than at any time before. Europe's industries excelled at churning out vast amounts of steel, textiles and chemical products and the continent's farmers had long since been able to produce enough food to feed vast numbers of non-agrarian workers. But despite the introduction of careful economic planning that coordinated wartime production, the demand for the military necessities of war inevitably outgrew supply.

A similar gap opened up in the 'civilian economy'. Since resources were diverted to military production, the needs of ordinary citizens could often no longer be met. Here, too, demand outgrew supply. The resulting increase in prices was dramatic and did not end with the war. Readjustment to peacetime patterns of demand was slow. Inflation remained a problem even after the war had ended: in 1920, consumer prices in Britain were almost two and half times what they had been in 1914. In France prices were nearly four times their pre-war level at this time, and by the end of the decade German prices had increased tenfold compared to 1914.

In order to return to the gold standard and re-establish the pre-war parity between gold and pound Britain needed to undo the process of wartime inflation at least partially. There was simply not enough gold in the vaults of the Bank of England to sustain the amount of money in circulation if the gold standard was reintroduced at pre-war parity. The volume of money in circulation had to fall and this could only be done if prices fell. In particular, the price of labour had to be reduced considerably. The Conservative prime minister Stanley Baldwin was quoted as saying: 'all the workers of this country have got to take reductions in wages to help put industry on its feet.'[1] Government later denied this version and insisted that Baldwin had only referred to workers in the coal industry. Nonetheless the thrust of economic policy was clear. Recovery was to be achieved through austerity for wage earners.

In preparation for a return to gold, the authorities embarked on a course of deflationary policies from the early 1920s: interest rates were raised and governments strove to present balanced budgets. The results were falling prices and wages, but also a dramatic increase in unemployment. These effects were felt very unevenly across different sectors of the economy. But overall, the results were devastating: in the early 1920s, 2 million Britons were looking for work. Britain's return to gold was associated with prospects that were far from golden for many workers. As a result, many contemporaries wondered whether the monetary restoration was worth the sacrifice. Some argued that a compromise could be found if Britain returned to the gold standard, not at the pre-war parity between pound and gold but at a new rate that reflected the post-war price levels. This would have avoided the necessity of lowering prices and wages. France took this less painful route, but in Britain this option was rejected in favour of the more orthodox solution.

A golden fetish

Perhaps the most striking fact about monetary debates in Britain in this period was that even the man who, in 1925, took the decision to re-establish the gold standard was not completely convinced that it made economic sense. At the time Winston Churchill (1874–1965) was not – yet – the iconic political leader that he later became. Rather he was an inexperienced minister of finance with a colourful political past. Under pressure from the political and financial establishment, he decided in favour of a return to gold. However, privately he vented his anger about the narrow-mindedness of many advocates of monetary orthodoxy: 'The Governor of the Bank of England shows himself perfectly happy with the spectacle of Britain possessing the finest credit in the world simultaneously with a million and a quarter unemployed.'[2] Later, he was even more explicit and called the decision to bring back the gold standard the worst of his political career.

The political and financial elites' attachment to gold was in many cases more rooted in sentiment than in reason. Barry Eichengreen, the foremost historian of the gold standard, speaks of a 'cultural condition' that underpinned the gold standard and that limited the ability of contemporaries to respond effectively to the economic challenges of the day.[3] In his collective biography of the leading central bankers of this period, Liaquat Ahamed describes them as having an 'almost theological belief in gold as the foundation for money'.[4] Only the most audacious economic commentators, equipped with superior self-confidence, dared to think outside the 'golden box'. The Swedish economist Knut Wicksell had already attacked the gold standard in the late nineteenth century and his compatriot Gustav Cassel had warned against the system's restoration after the war. But the most vocal and prominent critic of the institution in the post-war period was certainly Keynes. In his pamphlets and articles of the period, many of them now classics, he did not hold back with his attacks on the 'barbarous relic'.

Some, including Churchill, showed interest in this criticism. However, the reaction of most members of the establishment was closer to that of Montagu Norman, the governor of the Bank of England, who remained hostile to Keynes's unorthodox views. This resistance was not due to simple stubbornness. Rather, the arguments of defenders and critics of gold existed in parallel intellectual universes. Dialogue was ultimately impossible because of a lack of common ground. As Ahamed sums it up:

> What separated Norman from Keynes had less to do with economics and more to do with philosophy and worldview. For Norman, the gold standard was not simply a convenient mechanism for regulating the money supply, the efficiency of which was an empirical question. He thought about it in much more existential terms. It was one of the pillars of a free society, like property rights or habeas corpus, which had evolved in the Western liberal world to limit the power of government – in this case its power to debase money.[5]

There was no set of statistical data and no analytical argument that could have undermined faith in the gold standard. For many, this particular monetary arrangement had become part of the natural rights that formed the foundation of bourgeois society. The gold standard was part of a set of values that were neither in need of justification nor open to rational critique. The depth of the attachment may also be seen from Norman's reaction when Britain eventually abolished the gold standard again in 1931. He retreated to the countryside for several days to digest the blow and his friend Baldwin later recalled that 'going off the gold standard was for him as though a daughter should lose her virginity'.[6]

Nonetheless, it would be a caricature to depict the support for the gold standard as based entirely on the fetishism of hidebound elites. Tangible financial interests and economic arguments that were part of the period's intellectual orthodoxy equally contributed to paving the way for a return to monetary orthodoxy. To some extent the debate about the gold standard simply pitted social groups with different economic interests against each other: a return to gold at a new parity would have avoided the process of deflation that inflicted pain and abstinence mainly on wage earners and debtors. But under this alternative scenario creditors and banks would have suffered. The former would have lost – in 'gold terms' – part of their capital, and the latter some of the trust that the world put in them. It was clear to most contemporaries that a degree of economic suffering was inevitable as a consequence of wartime inflation. Many of the post-war political conflicts were over the question of which social groups ultimately had to pay for the cost of the war.

However, advocates of monetary orthodoxy did not see themselves as merely pursuing the narrow interests of one part of society to the detriment of another. Certainly, they argued, falling wages were bound to create some suffering in the short term, but this would be compensated for by the benefits of monetary stability in the longer term. Also, anyone listening to the economists of the time – among whom were a very few notable exceptions – would have been encouraged to expect that the high unemployment resulting from the government's policies was a passing phenomenon. The period of austerity for wage earners was a necessary adjustment, most economists were certain, that would quickly lead to full employment and renewed economic growth.

The reasoning was based on the notion of self-regulating markets, which, at this point, had been at the centre of economic analysis for well over a century. If demand and supply for a good were out of balance the price mechanism would make sure that balance was soon restored. The labour market was no different from any other market. If there was an excess of supply that manifested itself in unemployment, this simply meant that wages were too high to attract demand. Under such conditions, wage deflation was expected to set off a process of adjustment and recovery. Falling labour costs would lead to falling prices. This added to the purchasing power of households with cash holdings and the resulting increase in consumption was expected to contribute to economic recovery. Moreover, as the price of labour dropped, profits increased and with them savings and investment. With more savings available that could be turned into loans, interest rates fell and investment was sure to pick up. Additional demand and declining costs would lead to the creation of new businesses and the expansion of existing ones. Renewed economic growth and demand for labour would eventually lead to full employment again. Only very few economists questioned this reasoning.

However, the British economy stubbornly refused to behave as expected. Unemployment dropped from its peak in the early 1920s, but despite some fluctuations it remained at a high level. The unemployment rate reached a low point of 6.8 per cent in 1927, but for most of the period it remained much higher: until the beginning of the Second World War the number of Britons out of work never dropped below 1 million. At the same time, growth in Britain remained volatile and slow by international comparison. Export industries became less competitive. The return to gold at pre-war parity made British exports more expensive and industries that produced for domestic consumption suffered from the low level of demand that resulted from high unemployment. This protracted economic crisis was in contrast to a more positive development in other countries that had not reverted to gold at pre-war parity: the French economy recovered more quickly and outperformed the British for most of the 1920s and much of the 1930s.

To make matters worse, the politics of austerity also failed to achieve their main objective: monetary stability. Only six years after the return to the gold standard, Britain was forced off it again. Gold reserves were insufficient and despite emergency loans from the French and US central banks, the Bank of England succumbed to speculative pressure and announced the end to the gold standard. Contrary to the predictions of many economists, the end of monetary orthodoxy and the resulting devaluation of the pound marked the beginning of a sustained period of strong economic growth. The falling exchange value of the pound stimulated British exports and domestic demand was strengthened by low interest rates and growing real wages. The resulting economic recovery was one of the fastest in Britain in the twentieth century: unemployment dropped sharply.

In virtually all respects, the reintroduction of the gold standard failed to live up to expectations. Monetary stability, economic recovery and a return to full employment remained elusive. In the end, there was no economic reward for the hardship experienced by many Britons. In the light of this outcome, the economic policies deployed in this period and the theories underpinning them began to be increasingly questioned.[7] Contemporary mainstream economics had failed to predict and, worse, could not fully explain the economic developments of this period. It was not until 1936 that Keynes presented a fully developed alternative reading of what had happened.

Austerity, German style

In the meantime, the fatal consequences of Britain's flirtation with austerity did not stop politicians on the other side of the North Sea from resorting to similar measures in the pursuit of stability. When the Great Depression began, the German chancellor Heinrich Brüning (1885–1970) drastically cut government expenditure, increased taxes and undertook a series of measures designed to lower wages. Economically, the deflationary policies which he pursued from 1930 to 1932 were as damaging as their equivalent had been in Britain. The political harm, however, was far greater in Germany. Brüning's policies contributed directly to the failure of the Weimar Republic and to Adolf Hitler's rise to power.

Historians have often pointed out that Brüning's character predestined him to become a champion of austerity: he grew up in provincial Westphalia as the son of a pious vinegar merchant and, later in life, was known for his sour demeanour and ascetic lifestyle. However, we should not read too much into such biographical details. After all, Britain was prescribed a heavy dose of austerity by a politician who seemed a rather unlikely proponent of abstinence: Churchill was known to have a penchant for silk underwear, polo ponies and preferred champagne with his meals (which, when he ate at home, were served by one of his twenty-four servants).

If Brüning's biography can help in understanding the rise of austerity in Germany, the key lies more in his student years than in his childhood. As a young man, the future chancellor was an avid student of history and law. But the subject that most captured his imagination was economics. He studied the subject at some of the most renowned faculties of his time, including the London School of Economics (LSE) and graduated with the aim of becoming a professional academic. The First World War and his political commitments got in the way of this ambition, but after he was forced to flee from Germany in 1934, he eventually returned to his initial career plan and taught for several years at Harvard. Brüning was therefore well acquainted with the economic thinking of his day and his economic policy needs to be considered, at least in part, as an application of the principles which he had been taught in lecture halls and seminar rooms in Munich, Strasbourg, London and Bonn.

At the LSE and in Harvard, Brüning was a near contemporary of Schumpeter. It is not clear whether the two ever met, but Brüning was certainly acquainted with Schumpeter's views on Germany's economic situation. Schumpeter explained his diagnosis of the country's economic troubles in an article that was published shortly before the 1929 financial crash. Already at that time, Schumpeter argued that deflationary policies were urgently necessary in Germany. The economic boom of the 1920s, combined with powerful unions and strong left-wing parties, had led to a significant increase in wages and welfare expenditure. According to Schumpeter, this development led to serious economic risks. Beneath the surface of a booming economy, dynamics were already at work that would inevitably bring about a crisis. First of all, increasing wages led to a decline in the demand for labour. However, wage increases and redistributive taxes had another effect that was even more perilous: as profits were squeezed by powerful unions and politicians eager to please the masses, capital accumulation became insufficient. Profit earners were prevented from saving as much as before and, as a result, not enough capital was available for loans and investment. Absent a radical change of conditions, the lack of capital was bound to strangle economic growth.

However, could not working-class households compensate for this by saving more out of their increasing incomes? Schumpeter anticipated this objection and struck it down with a barrage of economic and cultural arguments. The working classes were unlikely to save because wage levels – even after the increases – remained low. Rather than saving any wage increases, they were bound to spend additional income. Also, and perhaps more importantly, they were culturally unsuited to saving. The ideal locus for saving was the 'industrial family'. Its members were 'trained to save' and in the habit of forgoing present pleasures in favour of future rewards. Workers, in contrast, could not be trusted to possess the same far-sightedness: 'as a group the working class thinks differently about these matters than the bourgeois world'.[8] Clearly, Schumpeter had read his Weber.

Since the working classes were not equipped with the wisdom to resort to the economically necessary abstinence of their own accord, abstinence had to be imposed on them. Wage increases needed to be limited or, if the damage had already been done, as in the German case, the pay of workers had to fall. The only hope for salvation from economic decline was austerity for wage earners. Already in 1929, Schumpeter recommended deflationary policies that very closely resembled the programmes enacted by Brüning in the following years.

From 1930, a series of measures was taken to lower wages. In collective wage and salary negotiations the government sided with employers and the government-led process of arbitration was systematically used to depress wage levels. In addition, a reduction in wages to 1927 levels was imposed by emergency decree in 1931. Public servants were subject to additional pay cuts and a special tax on their incomes. Other fiscal measures lowered the consumption of wage earners further. Indirect taxes on tobacco, alcoholic beverages and other consumer goods were substantially raised. At the same time, property taxes were reduced in order to stimulate capital accumulation. In order to reduce price levels and make the reduction in disposable income more bearable, the government put pressure on retail prices. The results were impressive: partly as a result of these policies, partly because of rising unemployment, prices and wages dropped substantially. However, none of the economic benefits that had been anticipated as a result manifested themselves. Unemployment remained high and economic growth low.

The politics of austerity

In part, Brüning's policies simply reflected the conventional wisdom of contemporary economists.[9] However, as the historian Bernd Weisbrod has argued, there was also a significant political and philosophical dimension to the economic policies pursued by Brüning and others in the last years of the Weimar Republic. From its inception the Weimar Republic was seen by many members of the economic elite as a semi-socialist 'trade union state' that, if left unchecked, would eventually suffocate free enterprise. This view was easily compatible with the economic arguments put forward by Schumpeter and others. But these concerns were much broader. At stake were not specific policies and their impact on economic indicators such as growth, employment, profits or wages, but fundamental questions about the nature and purpose of the state. In many instances, this conflict took the shape of a clash of political cultures and philosophical worldviews.

The socio-economic order of the Weimar Republic had been founded on a historical compromise between economic elites and trade unions. However, this accord was certainly not a love match. In 1918, after it had become clear that Germany had lost the war, the emperor packed his bags and escaped to the Netherlands. Worker and soldier councils – modelled on the Bolshevik example – were created everywhere and took over government. In a curious twist of fate, the first 'government office' to which Brüning was elected was the chairmanship of such a soldier council. However, this electoral success was due more to the respect he commanded as an individual than to any revolutionary leanings on his part.

While Brüning and his 'comrades' were still on the Western Front, two republics were proclaimed in Berlin. Karl Liebknecht declared a 'socialist republic', while the social-democrat Philipp Scheidemann called for the foundation of a 'German republic'. The more moderate current eventually prevailed. However, during the first days of the revolution the fear of political radicalisation led Germany's employers' associations to sign a historical accord with the trade unions that laid the foundations for many institutions which governed the social and economic life of the new republic. Named for its main signatories, the Stinnes-Legien agreement was a breakthrough for the trade unions: for the first time employers recognised them as the legitimate representatives of workers. Wage negotiations were henceforth to take the form of collective bargaining between unions and employers' associations and the results were to be universally binding. The agreement also contained more specific provisions that were equally ground-breaking. The most important were the creation of elected workers' councils that would function as representatives of employee interests within companies, and the introduction of the eight-hour day as a – frequently circumvented – norm.

Compared with the prospect of having their businesses nationalised by gun-toting Bolsheviks the agreement seemed preferable to many employers. But as the fear of radical revolution faded, many began to change their minds. Much of the instability of the Weimar Republic was the result of employers manoeuvring to get out of the concessions they had been forced to make in the early days of the republic.

Until the second half of the 1920s, the resistance of employers and their lobby groups was mainly passive. But when the economic recovery of the 1920s further improved labour's bargaining position, there was a growing feeling among employers that a stop needed to be put to the 'creeping nation-alisation' of their companies.[10] Like Schumpeter, employers saw increasing wages as a threat to profitability and competi-tiveness. But they also saw the rising tide of union power as a more fundamental threat. The incremental changes were seen as a tidal wave that would eventually lead to an outright attack on the principle of private enterprise and to the wholesale nationalisation of entire industries.

In 1928, employers decided that it was time put their foot down and take concrete steps to stem the red tide. Without waiting for the outcome of the annual wage negotiations, 160,000 workers of the steel and mining sector in the Ruhr area and other parts of north-western Germany were preventively served with redundancy notices in order to put pressure on the unions. Negotiations failed and the employers' association legally challenged the outcome of the arbitration process. By now, tens of thousands of workers were unemployed. Because of legal restrictions on unemployment benefits, the workers and their families could only rely on local charities for survival. As a result, public opinion began to turn against the employers and forced them to adopt a more conciliatory stance.

The conflict was eventually settled in a new round of mediation led by the government. In the event, employers had been unsuccessful with their radical stance and were forced to continue to work within the institutional framework of the much despised Weimar system. However, it also became clear in this conflict that the unions had only narrowly avoided defeat and mainly because they could count on the political support of the social democratic ministers in the coalition government. This experience only reinforced the view shared by many employers that a fundamental political change was required.

At the 1929 congress of the main industrial employers' association, all discussions about specific questions of detail were postponed. Instead, the whole meeting focused on questions of principle, and in particular on the existential threat to free enterprise posed by the political status quo. The contributions to the debate had titles such as 'German labour law: trailblazer of socialism' and 'Taxes as a tool for nationalisation'. But the main target of attacks was the concept of the 'democratic economy'. The term was used by the trade unions to promote the participation of workers in economic decisions through workers' councils and elected representatives. Employers saw this simply as a continuation of revolutionary Marxism by other means. As the president of the lobby group made clear in his introductory remarks, a defence against these tendencies could only be effective if it confronted them at the most fundamental level. The battleground was that of the 'great intellectual and political currents', and the outcome of these conflicts would 'affect the deepest roots of the state's essence'. Germany's 'political, economic and cultural development as a whole' would be shaped by the conflicts of the 1920s for 'epochs to come'.

Nothing less than a transformation on a par with the French Revolution could be expected – presumably including a great number of rolling heads – if the trade unions were not stopped. In accordance with this epic vision of the conflict, the German entrepreneurs claimed motives for their defence of free enterprise that reached far beyond narrow material interests. Only a free economy could lead to the 'fulfilment of all possibilities' and give 'leading personalities' the opportunity to fully develop their 'ideas and energy'. If collective political decisions interfered with free enterprise, this would not only threaten economic progress but also 'tear off the roots' of Germany's 'cultural development'. In order to drive home the point that German entrepreneurs were engaged in a conflict with epochal, perhaps eternal, consequences, two of the main interventions were made by a Protestant pastor and a Catholic theologian, who discussed the implications of the conflict between 'freedom' and 'structure' from a moral point of view.[11]

The exclusion from government of the Social Democrats now became the primary objective of many industrial lobby groups. They called for a 'common defence front' that would represent their interests by uniting all 'non-socialist politicians'.[12] Electoral arithmetic, however, made it clear that such a government could never be formed with parliamentary support. Its power would inevitably have to rest on presidential decree. The adoption of this logic by some of the most powerful lobbies in the country had a profound impact on Germany's political development from the late 1920s and contributed substantially to the creation of minority governments in the last years of the Weimar Republic, including Brüning's.

Seen in this light, the deflationary policies of the Brüning era no longer appear unambiguously as economically necessary measures, intended to restart economic growth and satisfy the obligations of war reparations. Instead, the policies were partly designed as a means to push back the power of organised labour and wipe out some of its past successes. Declining wages and increasing unemployment were not so much necessary evils on the way to economic recovery as the stick necessary to beat the trade unions. Seen in the larger context of Germany's development between the two world wars, it becomes clear that substituting the managed capitalism of the Weimar Republic with a social order built around more liberal values was as much an objective of the austerity policies of the 1930s as was restoring economic growth.

Both in Germany and Britain, the austerity policies of the interwar period were motivated by a mixture of economic, moral and political arguments. This was not peculiar to the European context. Americans conflated arguments that appealed to moral consciousness and rationality with equal ease. 'The remedy', a New York banker remarked after the outbreak of the financial crisis in 1929, 'is for people to stop watching the ticker, listening to the radio, drinking bootleg gin, and dancing to jazz; forget the "new economy" and prosperity founded upon spending and gambling, and return to the old economics and prosperity based upon saving and working.'[13] Abstinence, moral and economic, seemed to be the way forward.

In hindsight, the austerity policies of the period appear as a historic cul-de-sac. Only when contemporaries began to think beyond the orthodoxy of deflationary policies were the economic problems of the time solved. Britain recovered quickly after new economic policies allowed wages to grow and the pound to fall. The German debt crisis, in turn, was not solved by domestic thriftiness but by the intervention of the American president Herbert C. Hoover, whose initiative led to a suspension of debt and reparation payments.

On an intellectual level, the failure of austerity policies caused a caesura in the development of economic analysis. The theories that had underpinned the deflationary policies of this period had not stood up well in practice. The result was a process of relearning among economists that produced some of the most important works in the history of economics. Keynes wrote a guide to fixing the problems of capitalism, *The General Theory of Employment, Interest and Money* of 1936, a disillusioned Schumpeter predicted the end of capitalism in *Capitalism, Socialism and Democracy* of 1943 and Friedrich Hayek responded to both with a passionate defence of economic freedom in *The*

Road to Serfdom of 1944. In particular, the first and the third book also changed the way in which economists and lay people thought about abstinence and we will return to them in the two following chapters.

The failure of mainstream economics in this period turned out to be a blessing for the discipline because it stimulated the development of innovative theoretical frameworks. But the political price of this spectacular failure of economic analysis was high. In Britain and the United States the checks and balances of democratic government played an important role in correcting economic policies that were not producing the desired results. But in Germany, where austerity policies were imposed by an unelected government, all the stops were pulled out. The free fall of the German economy in this period proved to be too much for a political system that was already saddled with deep structural flaws. Misguided economic policies combined with a lack of commitment to democratic forms of government proved to be a fatal mix.

CHAPTER 5

Austerity can wait
Keynes

Economics was not the same after the Great Depression. A new perspective on abstinence was central to this paradigm shift. Previously economists had described saving as morally virtuous and economically necessary. But doubts emerged as a result of the economic experience of the 1920s and 1930s. A new, unorthodox analysis of the crisis put forward by Keynes and others suggested that excessive saving rather than unrestrained consumption was the root cause of economic stagnation. In this view, the Great Depression was not punishment for the vices of the Roaring Twenties but for excesses in the virtue of parsimony.

This analysis was a direct challenge to the conventional economic and moral wisdom of the time. Troubling questions that had not occupied centre stage since the time of Mandeville re-emerged: was the private virtue of saving really a threat to the public benefit of economic growth? From the late 1920s economic debates began to focus on what contemporaries called the 'dilemma of saving', a nexus later dubbed the 'paradox of thrift'. Keynes was clearly the key figure in these exchanges, but he was not the only or the first commentator to question the uncritical blessing that economists and moralists had bestowed on thriftiness. First, this chapter briefly examines pre-Keynesian versions of the paradox of thrift, before turning to Keynes's own views on abstinence and on the need for austerity in both the short and the long term.

The dilemma of saving before Keynes

In some respects, the 'dilemma of saving' was old hat when Keynes made it a central nexus of his analysis in the 1930s. Mandeville, Voltaire and others had argued long before that abstinence could be the right thing to do for individuals – morally and economically – and still be a curse for the economy. However, Smith and other classical economists had thought of a powerful comeback to this argument. Saving, they conceded, was money withheld from consumption and as such was capable of slowing down growth. However, savings also served an important function. They were turned into loans, which enabled entrepreneurs to invest. Savings were thus not unspent, but merely spent in a different way: rather than being spent on consumption goods, they ended up providing the funds for the acquisition of investment goods such as tools or machinery.

Neoclassical economists developed this argument further by showing that an imbalance between saving and investment was impossible: as in any other market, there was a supply (determined by the amount of savings available to be taken out as loans) and a demand (determined by investment opportunities). If savings were insufficient to meet the demand for loans, the price of loans, the interest rate, would go up and lead to higher savings and less investment. If the reverse were true, interest rates would go down, reducing the incentive to save but encouraging more credit-financed investment. Based on this reasoning, an excess of saving was impossible.

The main concern of pre-Keynesian economists such as Schumpeter was that insufficient savings could lead to prohibitively high interest rates that would choke off investment. Saving was therefore a crucial task and, as discussed in the last chapter, many believed that it was best entrusted to the groups in the population with the highest moral and intellectual standing. In the early nineteenth century only isolated voices asked whether, even after investments were taken into consideration, there might still be a risk of saving too much. Perhaps because of his generally gloomy disposition, or perhaps because of a keen intuition about the problems of the future, Robert Malthus (1766–1834) was one of the very few economic thinkers who questioned the optimism of his peers. 'Adam Smith', he wrote in 1821 to his friend David Ricardo, 'has stated that capitals are increased by parsimony, that every frugal man is a public benefactor, and that the increase of wealth depends upon the balance of produce above consumption. That these propositions are true to a great extent is perfectly unquestionable ...' But then he went on to ask whether Smith's analysis was valid in all circumstances. Making an essentially Mandevillean point he argued that 'the principles of saving, pushed to excess, would destroy the motive to production. If every person were satisfied with the simplest food, the poorest clothing and the meanest houses it is certain that no other sort of food, clothing, lodging would be in existence.' As he saw it, both insufficient savings and lack of consumption could be harmful for economic growth. 'There must be some intermediate point,' he concluded, 'where taking into consideration both the power to produce and the will to consume, the encouragement to the increase of wealth is the greatest.' Being a perennial pessimist, he added that 'the resources of political economy' might well not suffice to ascertain where this point of balance was.[1]

However, as Keynes argued later, 'Ricardo … was stone-deaf to what Malthus was saying'.[2] This was true for most economists of the nineteenth and early twentieth centuries. It is perhaps no coincidence that virtually all thinkers who dared to challenge the orthodox view on saving, including Malthus and later Keynes, did not hold economics degrees. Moreover, the first author to fully describe the dilemma of saving was no exception to this rule. John Mackinnon Robertson (1856–1933) had left school at age 13 and had no formal training in economics. Growing up on the Isle of Arran in a remote part of Scotland, he did not seem predestined for a career in the public eye. Nonetheless, he became a liberal Member of Parliament and well-known journalist with over twenty books to his name. One of his books, the *Fallacy of Saving* of 1892, contains what is considered to be the first complete statement of the 'dilemma of saving': 'Had the whole population been alike bent on saving, the total saved would positively have been much less, inasmuch as … industrial paralysis would have been reached sooner or oftener, profits would be less, interest much lower, and earnings lower and more precarious.'[3]

The point that Robertson was making went beyond the ideas of Mandeville and Voltaire in one important respect. Not only, he argued, would excessive saving lead to economic stagnation, but economic stagnation would in turn lead to a reduction in saving. Seen in this way, excessive levels of saving were not only a bad choice for the economy, but ultimately the level of saving was not a choice at all. Individuals could decide freely how much to save, but if collectively they 'flew too close to the sun' with their savings goals, then some of them would 'burn their wings'. Their income would fall, forcing them to reduce saving. As a result, the amount saved by *savers as a group* was not a matter of choice. It was set and enforced by inexorable economic mechanisms.

As Robertson himself acknowledged, the *Fallacy of Saving* was not a great success with readers. This was certainly due in part to the boldness of the thesis. For most Victorian readers the notion that saving could be anything but the pinnacle of civic and economic virtue seemed simply preposterous. As a lone voice against the mainstream of public opinion and of professional economists, Robertson's chances of being heard were slight. However, there were also problems with the way in which he put his argument. The nexus that he described may have been intuitively clear to those with some practical experience in economic matters, but he did not offer a formal counter-argument that proved the orthodox view wrong. He failed to explain why, in his scenario, overall saving was reduced by a fall in incomes and employment and not, as the economists of his time predicted, by a fall in interest rates.

If the bigger parts of the public became aware of the 'dilemma of saving' from the 1920s this was largely due to the efforts of two now largely forgotten Americans: William Trufant Foster (1879–1950) and Waddill Catchings (1879–1967). They had been classmates in Harvard in the last years of the nineteenth century. After that, their careers took them in different but complementary directions. Foster went on to attend Teachers College at Columbia University in New York and became an educational pioneer. Later he was appointed the first president of Reed College, a progressive liberal arts college on the west coast of the United States. Catchings graduated from Harvard Law School and became one of the most important bankers and captains of industry of the period. At different times, he was the director of several major corporations, including all-American companies such as Warner Brothers, Muzak Holdings, Studebaker and Chrysler. His business acumen was extraordinary, but also failed him on occasion: in 1930, he nearly bankrupted Goldman Sachs & Co., after distinguishing himself by becoming the first person appointed to run the bank who was not a relation of the founding families

Putting together their educational ambitions, first-hand experience in economic matters and financial muscle, the pair set out to convince the American public that a lack of consumer demand was the obstacle holding back growth in the United States. Large public works programmes funded by the state, they argued, were the only way out of the malaise. In order to popularise this message more effectively, Catchings founded and funded the Pollak Foundation of Economic Research. Foster became its first president.

Using the foundation as their principal vehicle, they began to disseminate their views in a series of books, articles and pamphlets with titles such as *Business without a Buyer* (1927), *The Road to Plenty* (1928) and *Progress and Plenty: A Way Out of the Dilemma of Thrift* (1930). The latter article was also reprinted as a small pamphlet under the title *The Dilemma of Saving* and distributed by the Pollak Foundation free of charge. Catchings and Foster used a full range of marketing strategies to create publicity for their ideas: in 1925 they offered a $5,000 cash prize for the best attempt to refute their arguments. A panel of prestigious economists awarded the prize and a selection of the essays was published by the foundation. Catchings and Foster acknowledged the validity of some of the criticism voiced in the essays, but in the rebuttal that was included in the volume they offered what they considered to be an improved and now irrefutable version of their argument.

The view that none of the essays had conclusively proven the theory of Catchings and Foster wrong was also shared by a young Austrian economist, Friedrich Hayek (1899–1992). Upon reading the volume, he decided to weigh in with an article of his own, in which he sought to prove the 'teachings of Mssrs. Foster and Catchings' wrong once and for all.[4] Hayek's stated ambition was also to counter a broader trend of increasingly more critical attitudes towards saving that was gaining traction in the 'quasi-scientific and popular literature' of the time. He clearly felt strongly about the matter. Although his piece was published in a scholarly journal, he started it on a personal note by explaining how he had 'recently witnessed the edifying spectacle of a "World Savings Day," on which central bank governors and ministers vied with each other in attempting to disseminate the virtue of saving'. This holiday, still celebrated by the thriftily minded everywhere on 31 October, was a recent innovation at the time: it had been proclaimed in 1924 at a congress of savings banks held in Milan. Given the worsening economic climate and the 'extensive financial backing' from which Foster and Catchings benefited, Hayek was concerned that they might ultimately be able to besmirch the virtuous idea of saving which he defended in his robust rebuttal. We will return to Hayek's views in the next chapter in more detail.

Despite Hayek's best efforts, the endeavours of Foster and Catchings enjoyed considerable success and have been credited with shaping contemporary public opinion in the United States and beyond. In particular, their work is said to have influenced Franklin D. Roosevelt's New Deal policies and some his most memorable speeches. The famous phrase 'one-third of a nation ill-housed, ill-clad, ill nourished' from the president's second inaugural address was almost a direct quote from a 1925 book by Foster and Catchings, *Profits*.[5]

Foster and Catchings did much to bring about a shift in public opinion and economic policies, but as Hayek and others had pointed out, they had not solved all the theoretical problems associated with the 'dilemma of saving'. This task was left to Keynes.

The *General Theory*

The publication of the *General Theory* was a crucial step in the development of economics. However, more important for the shift in economic policy that happened in this period were earlier publications by Keynes and the work of commentators like Foster and Catchings. 'Keynesian' economic policies had been introduced into the United States after Roosevelt's election in 1933, three years before the publication of the *General Theory*. In the same year, but under very different political auspices, Hitler adopted a policy of economic planning and large public works programmes in Germany, prompting the Keynesian economist Joan Robinson to remark that 'Hitler had already found how to cure unemployment before Keynes had finished explaining why it occurred'.[6]

Keynes described the 'dilemma of saving' – without using the term – in nearly the same terms as Robertson had three decades earlier:

For although the amount of his own saving is unlikely to have any significant influence on his own income, the reactions of the amount of his consumption on the income of others makes it impossible for all individuals simultaneously to save any given sums. Every such attempt to save more by reducing consumption will so affect incomes that the attempt necessarily defeats itself.[7]

Keynes did not add much to the description of the phenomenon, but he could explain why it occurred. Perhaps even more importantly, he outlined its full implications by embedding it in a comprehensive theoretical framework.

The key to understanding the 'mechanics' of the dilemma was to explain why, if savings and investment were not at unity, the adjustment process should happen through a decline in incomes rather than through a change in the rate of interest. That savings had to be equal to investments was not a matter of dispute between Keynes and orthodox economists: it is intuitively clear that only resources that are not 'eaten up' by consumption can be invested in machinery or other forms of capital. (The accounting unity can also be shown by three simple equations: income = consumption + investment; saving = income − consumption; therefore saving = investment.)

Keynes differed from other economists in the question of what mechanism made sure that this unity was achieved in practice. At the time, most economists believed that fluctuating interest rates would take care of this task. Keynes, in contrast, argued: 'the rate of interest is *not* the "price" which brings into equilibrium the demand for resources to invest with the readiness to abstain from present consumption'.[8] Unlike neoclassical economists he did not see interest as the 'reward for not *spending* on consumption. For him, interest was instead the 'reward for not-*hoarding*'.[9]

The distinction hinged ultimately on different assumptions about the psychology behind economic behaviour. Neoclassical economists believed that abstinence from consumption involved renouncing a pleasure and therefore commanded a reward. But for Keynes, interest was the reward for resisting another powerful urge, namely the urge to hold savings in ways that allowed savers to easily access them at any time they desired. This Keynes called 'liquidity preference'. Keeping all or a share of their savings in the form of readily accessible funds satisfied the desire of individuals to prepare themselves for unforeseen events. Cash stashed under the mattress or funds in a bank account, available at short notice, provided a sense of security. If necessary, individuals could use their funds immediately.

The degree of liquidity preference was determined by a combination of psychological disposition and real circumstances. The more insecure individuals feel, the greater their preference for liquidity. Seen from this perspective, the interest rate was the reward that needed to be paid to individuals to convince them to part with their liquidity. Savers needed to be convinced to hold their funds in ways that were less easily accessible, so that those funds could be more readily used to be loaned out. For example, the interest rate paid to a saver by a bank for holding cash in a savings account with a notice period of 30 days is, in a Keynesian view, not a reward for abstaining from the purchase of a new mobile phone. It is a reward to convince the saver to keep his or her funds in a 'less liquid' form compared to holding them in a current account or in a sugar bowl in the pantry.

Keynes's hypothesis had far-reaching consequences for economic analysis. If the level of interest was essentially determined by the triple balance between demand for loans, the liquidity preferences of savers and the supply of money, then it was no longer a price capable of bringing saving and investment into equilibrium. The rate of interest had no bearing on the amounts saved, but merely on the way in which savings were held.

Consequently, the amount of saving had to be regulated in a different way in order to ensure unity with investments. If a high liquidity preference prevailed, perhaps because of increased uncertainty about the economic or political future, this meant that interest rates – the reward for parting with liquidity – increased. If, as a result, less was invested then savings had to be reduced. Keynes argued that this would happen because the interest rate was now higher than the profits that could be expected from new investments. As a result entrepreneurs would not take out any more loans to finance new investments, output and employment would decline and with them incomes. And as incomes shrank, so the amount saved out of these incomes would be reduced. (Keynes assumed fixed propensities to save at any given level of income, at least in the short term.) In the end, after investment had declined, investment and saving were at unity again. Economic equilibrium was restored. But this came at a high price because equilibrium had been re-established at a lower level of output and hence employment. As in a satirical play, savers who started out with the best intentions, guided by virtue and economic prudence, brought on themselves economic decline and ultimately also the defeat of their own noble intentions. But, as Keynes pointed out in his discussion, 'virtue and vice play no part'.[10] Instead, the remorseless logic of economics ruled with an iron fist.

As a result, attempts to stimulate the economy by increasing savings, as suggested by Schumpeter and others, were futile. It was certainly possible to increase saving by redistributing income away from workers, with their low propensity to save, to the morally upstanding and frugal and above all more prosperous middle class. Additional efforts could be made to turn World Savings Day into a holiday popular beyond a small circle of bankers and Austrian economists. But this would do nothing to increase growth. So long as investment remained depressed, the economy would always gravitate towards a low-employment equilibrium.

For Keynes, there were only two ways out of a crisis of this type. One was to set interest rates at a sufficiently low level. In this way, entrepreneurs had access to loans at a rate of interest below the expected return on their investment. If the liquidity preference was high, then the central bank needed to increase the volume of money in order to lower the rate of interest. This policy was to be abandoned only after a level of investment had been reached that ensured full employment.

It was, however, possible that such monetary measures would be insufficient. If the expected return on investments fell to a very low point then even with interest rates near zero potential entrepreneurs might still prefer to sit on their money rather than invest it. Such behaviour could result from a number of conditions: low consumer demand and a resulting expectation that there was no market for additional output, a lack of technological innovation and hence of profitable investment opportunities, periods of extreme uncertainty such as wars or economic conditions when the general expectation was for prices to fall in the short term, meaning that a return on capital could be secured simply by delaying expenditure. In conditions like these – dubbed by later economists a 'liquidity trap' – monetary policy became ineffective.

In such cases, Keynes suggested, government had to step in directly. One way of doing this was to convince entrepreneurs to invest by creating opportunities that were simply too good to forgo. The example that Keynes used to explain the economic logic is now famous:

> if the Treasury were to fill old bottles with banknotes, bury them at suitable depth in disused coalmines which are then filled up to the surface with town rubbish, and leave it to private enterprise ... to dig the notes up again ... there need be no more unemployment, and ... real income ... and capital wealth ... would probably become a good deal greater.

Keynes added that paying entrepreneurs to build 'houses and the like' would be 'more sensible', but the economic effects were the same no matter what kinds of investment opportunities were created.[11] For Keynes economics was not a morality play. In the event, history proved him right: much of the additional government expenditure that helped end the Great Depression was not spent on 'sensible' things, but on fighting the most destructive war in human history.

For Keynes, as for Foster and Catchings, government intervention was the measure of choice to counteract economic downturns. Already in the 1920s he had first called for public works programmes to get the British economy out of its slump. Increasing the state's expenditure at a time when private consumption declined could help to solve the problem of excessive saving. Following this countercyclical logic the state was then to pay off the debts incurred in periods of economic crisis when the economy was booming. 'The boom,' Keynes wrote, 'not the slump, is the right time for austerity at the Treasury.'[12]

However, Keynes also warned that in the long term the state might be forced to play a role in planning investment beyond such anti-cyclical interventions. There were certain long-term trends that could make more permanent state intervention necessary. In a prosperous industrial economy the amounts of saving that needed to be matched by investment grew continuously. At the same time, growth of private consumption was increasingly slow. This was partly because prosperity had reached a level where the basic needs of many members of society were met. Moreover, population growth slowed down in most industrialised countries. Technological progress had often provided for lucrative investment opportunities and would continue to do so, but the timing and extent of innovation were uncertain.

Another problem resulted from the fact that investment decisions were based on *expected* rates on return. Keynes used the term 'expected' to draw attention to the uncertainty about the future associated with entrepreneurial decision-making processes. In this sense, investment would take place if entrepreneurs believed that a sufficient profit could be earned. But it may also be illuminating to read 'expected returns' in a different sense. Expectations reflect views about what *will* happen but also about what *ought* to happen. Entrepreneurs might therefore also hold back investment not because they fear that no profit can be earned but because the likely profit seems too low. Today, for example, corporations operating internationally may find that they can expect to make a profit on an investment in a mature industrialised economy in Europe, but the expected profits in emerging economies in Asia may be much higher. The likely outcome is a redirection of investment away from Europe despite the existence of profitable investment opportunities there.

As a consequence, Keynes expected 'to see the State … taking an ever greater responsibility for directly organizing investment'.[13] Admittedly, this line was only an aside and he was only thinking of 'organizing investment', perhaps in public–private partnerships. Full-scale nationalisation was not on his mind. However, even if ownership of businesses remained nominally private, who else but an all-powerful government planning department would be able to carry out the task of 'organizing investment'?

Was Keynes therefore a wolf in sheep's clothing or, rather, a Bolshevik cunningly disguised as an English gentleman? Or, more broadly speaking, to what extent did Keynes's views spring from a revolutionary analysis of economics or to what extent were they inspired by an attempt to change the world and make it a better place according to his own ethical and political convictions?

At first, Keynes appears as an economist and not much else. He certainly wanted to make the world a better place, but his route to doing that was characterised by a distinct lack of revolutionary ambition: greater efficiency in the utilisation of economic factors was what he was after. The problem which he sought to solve was that large quantities of economic resources lay idle while the basic material needs of many people were not met. Keynes, like anyone with a concern for economic efficiency, was preoccupied by the 'anomaly of unemployment in a world full of wants'.[14]

Unlike many contemporary socialists, Keynes did not want to solve this problem by fundamentally changing the way in which the economy worked. He did not want to defeat capitalism. Rather Keynes wanted to tweak it so that it worked as efficiently as he knew it could. Instead of dreaming up an ideal economic world, he was deeply committed to making the one that already existed work. In his own words, his aim was to 'indicate the nature of the environment which the free play of economic forces requires if it is to realize the full potentialities of production'.[15]

Keynes wanted economies to grow their way out of want. Therefore he only ever contemplated redistribution of incomes as a measure to regulate the savings rate. Like Schumpeter, he was convinced that families with higher incomes tended to save more than those on lower incomes. Keynes did not attribute this so much to a moral disposition as to the simple fact that the basic needs of humans are finite and that saving therefore tended to increase once income rose over and above a certain threshold. As a result, one way to reduce the potentially harmful effects of excessive savings was to redistribute income from rich to poor.

However, for Keynes this was merely a logical consequence of his economic analysis. It was not an ethical imperative, like the Christian obligation to charitable giving. This type of social redistribution Keynes rejected, based on economic and cultural arguments borrowed from Edmund Burke: mainly he believed that taking from the rich to help the poor would not work because the poor outnumbered the rich so vastly. Moreover, Keynes agreed with Burke that only wealthy citizens could bring certain advantages to the cultural life of a society. Therefore, social equality was bound to lead to cultural decline.[16] Keynes was much more of an elitist and much less of a bleeding heart than he has often been made out to be.

It should also be emphasised that Keynes's views on the overall size of government were entirely pragmatic. He saw the state as a tool to achieve certain economic ends and had no dogmatic views about whether a bigger state was intrinsically better than a smaller one. In times of economic crisis government was to expand, in times of boom it could shrink. Also in the long term, the size of government was not a matter of principle but of economic utility.

Pragmatic realism was a distinctive feature not only of Keynes's theoretical outlook, but also of the method that led him to his revolutionary revision of economic analysis. Modern economics was not concerned with morality as such and many nineteenth-century social reformers criticised it for its allegedly corrosive effects on ethical standards. Nonetheless, classical economics still operated with assumptions about economic behaviour that were often utopian. Smith, like all self-respecting thinkers of the Enlightenment, expected individuals to behave rationally. And where they were not acting rationally, living in a world that the Enlightenment had created was expected to make them rational creatures who acted in accordance with the rationally devised institutional frameworks of modernity. To a large extent this educational process was successful: economic rationality became a pervasive motivation of human action and the institutional vestiges of pre-capitalist societies withered away quickly. As a result, the classical theories of economics were, by and large, successful at predicting economic outcomes.

Where modern economic theory failed, Keynes argued, this was to a large extent due to an idealised vision of human motives and behaviour. He criticised orthodox economics for the assumption that 'at any given time facts and expectations were ... given in a definite and calculable form'. Reality was very different from these idealised assumptions. Despite the progress of rationality, the future remained to a large extent unknowable. Ignorance and uncertainty were the pervading features of economic decision-making. Keynes was categorical: 'we have, as a rule, only the vaguest idea of any but the most direct consequences of our acts.'[17] There was near complete uncertainty about economic developments even in the medium term of 30–40 years, a time horizon relevant to many invest-ment decisions. The calculus of probabilities may have been able to shed light on tomorrow's weather, Keynes pointed out in the 1930s, but it could not help anyone to know the economic conditions in 1970. 'About these matters there is no scientific basis on which to form any calculable probability whatever. We simply do not know.'[18]

Aware of our ignorance but still forced to take decisions with long-term consequences, we tend to attach the greatest importance to the flimsiest guesswork that helps to cover up our ignorance, Keynes argued. The prevalent strategy becomes to guess what others are guessing about the future. However, the resulting predictions are more a fig leaf to cover collective ignorance than accurate forecasts. In Keynes's view, much of economic theory not only ignored the reality of uncertainty, it was in itself part of the attempt to cover it up: 'I accuse the classical political economy of being itself one of these pretty, polite techniques which tries to deal with the present by abstracting from the fact that we know very little about the future.'[19] The role that opaque financial instruments and rapidly shifting economic expectations have played in the current economic crisis has done much to remind economists of the importance of Keynes's thoughts about uncertainty.

Classical and neoclassical economists had written about economic men and women as they ought to be: rational, well-informed and prudent. But Keynes wrote a theory about men and women as they really were: ill-informed, subconsciously aware of their ignorance and always prone to be carried away by irrational fears and hopes. Mandeville and his contemporaries had made enormous progress in understanding economic mechanisms by putting to one side the question of how humans *ought* to act and by asking instead how they *really* acted. In a similar way, Keynes attempted to leave the brave and perhaps utopian assumptions of earlier economists behind and replace them with a more realistic view. This enabled him to arrive at a better understanding of economics and it also freed him and his theory from the utopian aspirations and moral judgements implicit in earlier theorising.

The long run

Finding practical solutions to the economic problems faced by the men and women of his time was Keynes's primary concern. Economic dogma and the intellectual sophistication of economic analysis interested him only in so far as they contributed to this end. In this 'presentism', the influence of Burke may be felt again. The famous conservative rejected the notion that accepting sacrifices in the present could be a road to future benefits. Burke's formative experience was the French Revolution, in which bloodshed and violence were justified as a necessary stepping-stone on the way to a better and more humane society. The classical theory of saving, which Keynes attacked so vigorously, constructed just such a nexus between present sacrifice and future benefit.

Hayek later criticised Keynes harshly for this alleged concentration on 'quick fixes': '[Keynes] stopped thinking about what, in the long run is desirable'.[20] This accusation was, however, not entirely fair. Keynes was more than a 'practical man' whose main ambition was to grease the wheels of capitalism as effectively as possible in the short run. He cared about the long term and expressed strong views not only about the means, but also about the ends of economic development. In Keynes's time, as today, economic growth was considered to be a goal in itself by most economists and capitalists. But that was not Keynes's view. For him, as for Aristotle, the 'love of money' could never be a goal in itself. Wealth was only a means, not an end. What, then, was the ultimate purpose of human existence for Keynes? Most 'Keynesianists', including Victoria Chick and Robert Skidelsky, use the Aristotelian term of the 'good life' to describe what Keynes saw as the ultimate goal which individuals and humanity as a whole should strive for. The philosopher George Edward Moore, a Cambridge contemporary with a major influence on Keynes, described the main ingredients of the good life as 'friendship and the contemplation of beautiful objects'.[21]

However, as Aristotle had pointed out, 'neither life itself nor the good life is possible without a certain minimum supply of the necessities'.[22] Keynes was well aware of this. He knew that for most of his contemporaries preoccupations with the material needs of life were bound to get in the way of leading the good life. He therefore resorted to a redemptive perspective:

the prevalent concern of humanity would be with the satisfaction of material wants for another century or so. After that, mankind – at least to the extent that it lived in the more advanced economies of the globe – would enter a new stage of existence. Material want would be a thing of the past and humans would devote themselves to new priorities. To Keynes, his own times, in which humanity struggled with 'the problem of want and poverty and the economic struggle between classes', were 'nothing but a frightful muddle, a transitory and unnecessary muddle'.[23]

This notion of a period of toil followed by redemption in a better world, free of want and oppression, was well-trodden ground for most of Keynes's readers, at least to those who were familiar with the traditions of Christianity and Communism. However, for Keynes neither Doomsday nor world revolution was required for the transition to a better world. The progress of productivity was enough. Humanity would be able to produce vastly more with far less effort, thus solving the 'economic problem' and releasing mankind into a new age in which men and women would work less and devote themselves to leading the good life. Keynes expected that a three-hour working day would become the norm in this future paradise. This prediction may have been to some extent rooted in his personal experience. As a young graduate he had worked at the India Office. The working hours there, 11 o'clock to 5 o'clock with an hour for lunch and two months of holidays, had left him plenty of time to pursue other interests.

However, technological progress alone was not enough to bring about the transition to an age of contentment. Keynes distinguished two classes of human needs: a first class of 'absolute' needs that we feel irrespective of the conditions in which other men and women live, and a second class of needs that arises from our tendency to compare ourselves with others. The first class of needs was finite and the progress of productivity would eventually take care of them, but the second class was potentially infinite. As Veblen had pointed out, conspicuous consumption had been a central feature of human societies since earliest times. One of its principal purposes was to outdo others and continuously re-enact social superiority. This type of consumption was potentially limitless because it did not satisfy a need but merely served to demonstrate a greater ability to spend compared to others.

Fundamental shifts in human habits and behaviour were therefore necessary, in addition to the progress of productivity, to enter a new era of abstinence from growth. Keynes was confident that this could be done: 'We shall use the new-found bounty of nature quite differently from the way in which the rich use it to-day, and will map out for ourselves a plan of life quite otherwise than theirs.'[24] This was an ambitious objective. It required that humanity collectively underwent a 'Rousseau moment' and realised that life for others and through others could only lead to a corrupt rather than a good life. And as Rousseau had pointed out, such a transformation would also require a fundamental change in the political structure. Under the corrupt regime of never-ending material wants, the main purpose of the state was to protect private property. If this purpose withered away because there was no scarcity anymore, a new form of social contract would have to underpin political organisation.

In a similar way, social cohesion would have to be set on a new footing. Veblen had drawn attention to the important function that the attempts of the poor to emulate the consumption of the rich have in unequal societies. No matter how futile, the hopes of the majority to become like the rich, or at least like those who were slightly better off than themselves, were a crucial component of the glue that held together otherwise deeply fractured societies. Communities that were free of all forms of want would not be able to rely on this mechanism anymore and would have to find different forms of social organisation. Keynes foresaw that the social life of the future would be based once again on the 'most sure and certain principles of religion and traditional virtue'.[25] Almost inevitably, broadly shared access to economic resources and political power would have to be part of the social contract after the end of growth.

However, what would give individuals and society a sense of purpose once the centuries-old motivation of material gain had faded away? Keynes admitted that it would be a 'fearful problem' for the 'ordinary person with no special talents' to find ways to fill their day once the necessity of toil was removed. He therefore advised that societies should encourage the 'arts of life' and the 'activities of purpose' even while humanity was still travelling in the 'tunnel of economic necessity'.[26]

Keynes was not the only contemporary who believed that humanity could kick its greedy habits. In 1938, Sigmund Freud's disciple Otto Fenichel published an article 'The drive to amass wealth' in the *Psychoanalytic Quarterly*. The piece discussed the deeply rooted and broad-ranging psychological needs that were satisfied by the accumulation of wealth. However, Fenichel also concluded that while the structure of these psychological needs could not be altered, the ways in which they were satisfied were essentially determined by the social and historical context. For example, only in societies where social recognition and power were tied to wealth would individuals attempt to satisfy their inborn narcissism by accumulating riches. In societies where the arts were held in high esteem, such as the one which Keynes envisaged for the future, dedicating time to perfecting one's flute skills was bound to go as far in ensuring the 'narcissistic supply' as piling up more material possessions. It seemed perfectly possible that everyone, not only Cambridge dons like Keynes, would be able to learn how to lead a life that revolved around intellectual and artistic achievement, friendship, contemplation and the pursuit of higher moral values.

Meet the Keyneses

There are two distinct Keyneses: one an economist concerned with maximising growth in the short and medium term, and one a moral philosopher who preaches the end of growth and abstinence from consumption. In each of his incarnations Keynes's thought is part of different intellectual traditions. As an economist, he builds on the coolly rational tradition of Mandeville and the concomitant disregard for moral categories. As a moral philosopher, he writes in the tradition of Mandeville's opponents. Traces of the ideas of Aristotle, Rousseau and Veblen can be found in Keynes's vision for the long term.

Keynes resolves the tension between his economic and moral arguments by assigning them to different epochs of human development. He was enough of a practical man to know that preaching abstinence in his age naively disregarded a reality in which many were still suffering from want. But philosophical enquiry and perhaps personal experience had also taught him that there was a limit to how far consumption of material goods was necessary and a source of satisfaction. Keynes and many of his friends in the famous Bloomsbury set were fortunate enough to be free of material concerns. Their privileged social position meant that they could dedicate themselves to higher aims and find fulfilment in artistic and intellectual pursuits. One might say that it was an extension of the Bloomsbury set's lifestyle to all of humanity that Keynes had in mind for the future.

Whether or not this was a realistic outlook remains open to debate. Keynes and his friends had been born into positions of privilege. They didn't have to 'unlearn' the preoccupation with material gain in the way that humanity would have to in order to enter Keynes's new era. How exactly such a radical transformation of values could be brought about was never made clear by Keynes. He seemed to believe that educational measures deployed while humanity was still travelling in the 'tunnel of material want' would suffice. Against this view, conservative critics are bound to argue that such a transformation is impossible and contrary to human nature. The objection from the radical left would inevitably be that a change of such proportions requires a revolution, perhaps even a global one.

The other question that Keynes does not address is how to ensure that the bounty of increasing productivity would be distributed in a fair manner in society in the future. That he and his Bloomsbury friends could live free of economic concerns was in part due to the unequal distribution of wealth in early twentieth-century Britain. Their incomes from trust funds and Keynes's short working hours in the civil service were made possible by the hard toil and low standards of living of many workers in Britain and its colonies. The progress of productivity could do much to improve the lot of the majority, but if the problem of distribution was not solved most of the gains of rising productivity could be skimmed off by predatory elites. Perhaps Keynes assumed that the increase of wealth would be so great that even the smaller shares of the pie would become sufficiently large to end all economic worries. Or perhaps he expected a gradual equalisation of distribution. However, he left himself open to the charge of naivety because he failed to explain in any detail how the transition between the economic age of the present and the moral age of the future could be brought about.

Many of these wider issues in Keynes's work were never fully explored because the interest in Keynes the moral philosopher remained far more limited compared with the attention devoted to his alter ego, the quick-fix economist. It was Keynes the economist who became a towering intellectual figure. His analysis had proven its power by guiding the Western world out of the Great Depression and the economic troubles caused by the Second World War into a period of unparalleled economic stability and prosperity. Austerity now seemed to be a thing of the past, both as an economic condition and as an economic idea.

CHAPTER 6

Austerity for the state
Hayek

In the 1930s, the greatest crisis in the history of capitalism was overcome by consuming more rather than less. As if that was not enough to discredit traditional views about the benefits of abstinence, the decades after the Second World War became a golden era which combined high economic growth and rapidly increasing individual consumption. Europeans began to be able to afford cars, television sets and holiday trips, and Americans started to buy second cars, colour TVs and air travel. Even the socialist countries experienced substantial growth – sometimes outperforming the West – and saw a consumer revolution of a kind. In a virtuous cycle, more consumption seemed to beget more prosperity. In part, the boom was fuelled by the voracious appetite of European consumers who had been deprived of many comforts during the war and whose wages grew steadily. Moreover, European industries were catching up with American levels of productivity, making consumer goods more affordable. Nothing could seem more démodé in this new age of affluence than those preaching thrift and restraint. Economists who continued to teach the neoclassical doctrines about saving often did so in front of empty lecture theatres, while Keynesian scholars attracted students in droves.

However, the dominance of Keynesian economics began to crumble when, from the early 1970s, Western economies experienced slow growth, increasing unemployment and inflation. The tide of economic discontent swept into power a new generation of politicians in the mould of Margaret Thatcher (1925–2013) and Ronald Reagan (1911–2004). They were inspired by monetarist economics and the neoliberal thought of Friedrich Hayek (1899–1992) and their views on consumption and abstinence were radically different from those of their Keynesian predecessors. Private saving was once again seen as an economic virtue and a stimulus for investment rather than as an obstacle to growth. However, most importantly, the new economic orthodoxy recommended a heavy dose of abstinence to the state.

Government budgets across the Western world had grown rapidly since the 1930s. This was partly a result of the Second World War and the subsequent Cold War, and partly the consequence of expanding welfare systems. In the United States, expenditure by the federal government was equal to 3.4 per cent of GDP in 1930. In 1945, this had surged to 41.9 per cent. The end of the war brought spending down to a low of 11.6 per cent in 1948. But the drop did not reach pre-war levels and by 1960 expenditure had climbed to 17.8 per cent, increasing further to 19.3 per cent in the following decade. The development in many other Western countries was similar. Looking at any chart of UK government spending during the twentieth century, two peaks are clearly visible. Each of them marks a world war. But apart from these extraordinary events there is a long term trend of increasing expenditure that is also visible in the interwar period. This development continued after the Second World War until the late 1970s.

Growing government budgets were not spent wholly on consumption goods. States also invested in infrastructure and, in some cases, even became the owners of businesses and entire branches of industry. Nonetheless, a substantial part of growing government expenditure was on forms of collectively organised consumption that ranged from strategic bombers and nuclear submarines to health care and elementary school teaching. In addition, governments also increasingly funded payments to the unemployed, pensioners and other welfare recipients and hence forms of individual consumption.

The new generation of right-wing politicians attempted to reverse this trend and to reduce the size of the state by introducing policies that resemble today's austerity policies in many respects. In practice, national experiences varied greatly and not all forms of state expenditure were reduced with the same verve, or at all: welfare cuts were usually a central element, while other forms of expenditure, such as military spending, were often spared from cuts or even expanded. Consequently, the economic results of the new policies differed. In the US, overall government expenditure grew substantially and much of the economic recovery of the 1980s was due to the 'weaponized Keynesianism' of the Reagan years. In the UK, where government spending actually fell, the result was a deep and prolonged crisis.

The intellectual case for the new policies was based on a mix of arguments. Monetarist economics was a component, as were the economic principles of traditional liberalism. However, perhaps the most important inspiration came from Hayek's neoliberalism. Strikingly, this new brand of liberal economic thought did not mainly focus on considerations of economic efficiency. The preservation of liberty as an ethical imperative was at the centre of Hayek's reasoning. Instead of worrying about the maximisation of output, Hayek asked how individual liberty could be defended against the growth of tyrannical states. The economic implications of his arguments were far-reaching but his objectives were ethical and political in nature.

Paradoxically, the revolution in economic thinking of the 1970s was therefore as much the result of the historical experience of the twentieth century and of philosophical traditions of the nineteenth century as of the new forms of economic analysis. The political nature and the deep historical roots of neoliberal arguments are nowhere clearer than in Hayek's writings. This chapter therefore focuses first on the evolution of his thought in the 1930s and 1940s, and then on the factors that made his views politically influential from the mid-1970s.

An Austrian in London

Hayek wrote most of his important contributions after he had left his native Vienna in 1931. At first he settled in London, having been appointed at the LSE, then he left for Chicago in 1950 to take up a position at the University of Chicago. There he remained until 1962 when he returned to Europe, taking up a position at the University of Freiburg in Germany. In London and Chicago he wrote his two most influential works: *The Road to Serfdom* of 1943 and the *Constitution of Liberty* of 1960. In 1975, the year she became leader of the Conservative Party, Margaret Thatcher is said to have pulled the latter book out of her bag and slammed it on the table at a meeting of the party, exclaiming 'This is what we believe!'[1] In this period, Hayek became an inspirational figure to conservative leaders in the UK and elsewhere. On his ninetieth birthday, Thatcher wrote to thank him for 'the leadership and inspiration that your work and thinking gave us'. The admiration was mutual. After Hayek had first met Thatcher in 1975, he remarked: 'She's so beautiful.'[2]

However, the prominent position into which Hayek and his writings were propelled in the 1970s and 1980s should not obscure the fact that he was a marginal figure when the books were written. Hayek's anti-Keynesian views together with his thick Austrian accent made sure that his lectures at the LSE were intimate gatherings. Rather than feeling inspired, students ridiculed him: his frequent references to the economic importance of the fluctuations of relative prices earned him the nickname 'Mr Fluctooations'.[3]

In the academic and political debates of the time, Hayek was on the losing side. Keynes's influence on public opinion in the UK and beyond was growing. An increasing share of the public became convinced that excessive consumer abstinence was the cause of the economic crisis and that only increased government expenditure could offer a cure. Hayek opposed both notions. However, the criticism that he expounded in his article against the 'teachings of Mssrs Foster and Catchings' and elsewhere did not resonate in academic circles or with the wider public. In an attempt to influence public opinion and counteract Keynes's dominance, he, Lionel Robbins and other prominent LSE economists wrote a letter to the editor of *The Times* of London in 1932. Theirs was a direct response to a letter written by Cambridge economists, led by Keynes, calling for increased private consumption and expanding government budgets.

Nothing, Hayek and his colleagues argued, could be more pernicious than doing what Keynes had asked the public to do in his letter: desist from saving. Hayek and his colleagues agreed that a lack of investment was causing the crisis. Increased saving was required to provide the necessary funds for this end. Calling for increased private consumption would have the contrary effect and depress investment still further. 'It is perilous in the extreme,' they warned against the Keynesian siren calls, 'to say anything which may still weaken further the habit of private saving.'[4]

The other controversial issue was whether or not deficit-financed public works programmes could contribute to restoring economic growth. Hayek and his friends argued that instead of providing economic stimulus such additional expenditure was bound to drive up interest rates. They also predicted that other, unspecified, economic friction would result, further reducing investment. The economic logic behind these arguments was not explained in the short letter, but the expectation of rising interest rates was most likely based on a version of the 'loanable funds' theory. According to this view, an increase of public deficit spending would up the demand for loans. If saving did not increase to the same extent, the price for loans, the interest rate, would go up. The resulting process would today be called 'crowding out': private investors who were unable to pay the higher interest rate would desist from investing in profitable projects, while potentially unprofitable public investments and state-funded consumption would increase because their extent was not limited by considerations of profitability. Public works programmes therefore not only put a brake on private investment, but also distorted the competitive logic of the market. Detrimental effects for economic development in the long term were inevitable.

The arguments of Hayek and his friends were hardly new. They did their best to present them in a fresh and appealing way, but in substance they were re-proposing the views which mainstream economists had held for some time at this point. As we have seen, Schumpeter was peddling similar views in Germany around this time. However, as the crisis continued the persuasive power of such ideas dwindled. Long before Keynes delivered the theoretical 'knock-out blow' in his *General Theory* the public had lost faith in the prescriptions of mainstream economics. In the US and elsewhere political movements that promised to ignore the advice of orthodox economists rapidly gathered force.

Many of today's economists agree that the laissez-faire advice imparted by orthodox economists in the 1930s was misguided. The view of Milton Friedman – not suspected of Keynesian leanings – deserves to be quoted at length:

If you go back to the 1930s, which is a key point, here you had the Austrians sitting in London, Hayek and Lionel Robbins, and saying you just have to let the bottom drop out of the world. You've just got to let it cure itself. You can't do anything about it. You will only make it worse. You have Rothbard saying it was a great mistake not to let the whole banking system collapse. I think by encouraging that kind of do-nothing policy both in Britain and in the United States, they did harm.[5]

No reply

When the *General Theory* was published in 1936 Hayek did not comment publicly. He had written a critical review of Keynes's earlier *Treatise on Money* and he had not shied away from taking on Foster and Catchings. Keynes had even sent Hayek advance copies of the *General Theory* to allow for a quick reply. But, in the words of Nicholas Wapshott, Hayek was a 'no show' to this duel.[6]

However, to suggest that Hayek simply chickened out is misleading. Hayek did write a powerful reply to Keynes: *The Road to Serfdom*. The whole book is a damning indictment of Keynesianism but it is not an attack on Keynes's economics. Hayek mounted his counter-attack by warning of the political, philosophical and psychological long-term consequences of Keynesianism. In the same way in which Mandeville and Voltaire had shifted the argument away from the moral plane towards economics in order to mount a more powerful defence of luxury, Hayek shifted the debate away from economics.

A reader unaware of the economic debates of the period might be forgiven for seeing *The Road to Serfdom* first and foremost as a history book in the style of the moralising historians of antiquity who wrote as much to teach lessons to the living as to explain the events of the past. Having witnessed the devastations caused by the rise of the Nazi movement in Germany, the question that Hayek asked was 'How could this have happened?' and, in a second step, 'Could it happen again?' Hayek's main concern was to point out that, in contrast to what some of the war propaganda suggested, there was nothing inherently German in the rise of the Nazi movement. Other societies, he argued, might just as easily degenerate into authoritarian dictatorships if they did not learn the lessons from what had happened in Germany. His book was a warning to future generations not to take this danger lightly despite the fact that it had become clear at the time he was writing that the Axis powers could not win the war.

Hayek's take on the question of how Germany had descended into fascism differed in important respects from the understanding of many of his contemporaries. At the time, many saw fascism as a counter-movement to the increasing strength of left-wing parties. Today, many historians adopt a similar perspective: social and economic elites began to withdraw their support for Weimar democracy because they were convinced that the Weimar Republic was a Trojan horse that would eventually allow trade unions and socialists to take over power.

Hayek's perspective reversed the received narrative. Fascism, to him, was the fulfilment of a socio-economic development that began during the Weimar Republic, not a counter-reaction. During the Weimar years, socialists had promoted state intervention and the aim of a 'democratic economy'. In Hayek's view, this had prepared the political structures and the mindset of the German people for the assault on liberty carried out by the Nazis. Socialists and liberal reformers were committed to democracy and did not intentionally undermine liberty. But their attempts to plan and regulate economic development nevertheless gradually reduced individual freedom. Building on these foundations, the Nazis could easily erect an order in which individual freedom counted for nothing and the directions of a powerful state for everything. Far from being opposites, socialists and fascists were united by their passion for planning. If they fought bloody battles on the streets this was only because they were competing for the same groups in society: those who were attracted by the comforting message that the state would take care of solving society's problems.

Like Keynes, Hayek was asking how humans reacted to insecurity. For Hayek, the precarious conditions of the period led to an increasing tendency to put the state in charge of creating order by planning and coordinating. Keynesianism was but one of the many manifestations of this tendency. Left-wing parties were particularly keen on planning, but it was a 'passion' that could be found across the political spectrum. Hayek did not deny that state intervention could result in increasing economic efficiency. Planners might actually make good on their promise to put an end to the paradox of unused economic resources and persistent want. But the price for such quick economic fixes was high. As had happened in Germany, those who tried to solve the economic problems of their times unwittingly put the economic future at risk and set off a process of change that could ultimately undermine individual liberty. The road to serfdom, it might be said, was paved with the best intentions of the best economists.

In the pursuit of better economic outcomes, states in this period used a variety of tools. The most hotly debated in the 1930s were deficit-financed public works programmes. Often such projects took the form of public investment in infrastructure projects such as roads, bridges or reservoirs. States could also boost investment expenditure by nationalising companies and altering their investment strategies. In theory, investment decisions of firms and private individuals could also be controlled by the state while private ownership was maintained. Keynes had contemplated similar solutions for the future. However, Hayek warned that this kind of separation was illusory. Where the decisions about investment were taken out of private hands, property in productive capital itself would soon follow suit.

Another method for the state to plan a way out of an economic slump was to boost consumption expenditure. This could happen by purchasing goods for use by the community. Examples were the creation of a larger and better equipped military, a better resourced health service and better schools, or subsidies for public transport. States could also boost demand by subsidising individual consumption through payments to the unemployed, pensioners and other welfare recipients. Tax breaks for those with an income could often achieve much the same effect. All of these measures, if financed by public deficits, were bound to increase demand and hence stimulate investment and growth.

Hayek's concern with such measures was not mainly that they might not produce the intended outcomes of stimulating economic growth and reducing unemployment. Indeed, he thought it likely that they would. But the very mechanisms that made planning work in the short term defeated its purpose in the long term. In a market economy, the fluctuations of relative prices functioned as an information system. When private individuals had to take decisions about where to invest, what profession to study for, what to buy or what to produce, they could not possibly know about all the criss-crossing economic decisions of thousands, perhaps millions of individuals that were relevant to their own decision. Faced with a high degree of complexity individuals could use relative prices as a means of orientation.

Prices are simple to read and yet highly sensitive indicators of economic change. Rising prices of black cloth may lead

producers in England to invest in its production, even if they
do not know anything about the causes of the added demand.
Changing fashions in China, periods of mourning in Brazil, or
health fads in Australia might be involved. But textile producers
do not need to become fashion critics, anthropologists or
doctors familiar with local conditions in distant places in order
to react appropriately. They only need to observe the changes
in the price of black cloth relative to other goods. Prices, it
might be said, are the nervous system of capitalism, transmitting millions of impulses at incredible speed.

State intervention distorts this system and prevents it from
transmitting accurate information. This is not an avoidable
side-effect. It is the very purpose of the state's intervention to
direct factors of production like labour or capital to 'go where
they would not normally go'. When the state decides to build
a dam, it artificially creates demand for labour and investment
goods where there would be none in a purely private economy.
When the state spends money on defence and health care, it
artificially creates demand. And when the state offers welfare
provision to the unemployed, this distorts the signals normally
given by different wage levels about the usefulness of different
professions to society. The common result of these different
interventions is that individuals take decisions about investments, careers, consumption and other economic matters based
on a false impression of reality.

Tampering with the monetary base had a similarly distorting
effect. If the state followed Keynes's advice, it needed to
counter the effects of the increased liquidity preference by
increasing the supply of money. But in Hayek's view this
would merely create inflation, which distorted relative prices
and provided a strong disincentive to private saving. Balanced

budgets and low inflation were therefore high on the list of political objectives which Hayek recommended.

In the short term, deficit spending and monetary manipulations could bring positive economic results, but in the long term they limited the ability of economies to adapt in an evolutionary manner to new challenges. Crucially, Hayek did not believe that the decisions of private individuals, left to their own devices, always produced the best outcomes. This was a central difference between his ideas and those of classical liberal economists such as Mill. Classical liberals – sometimes referred to as 'paleo liberals' by Hayek's friends – had assumed that free markets produced economic equilibrium and led to optimal utilisation of economic resources. But Hayek and his generation of 'neoliberals' moved on from this notion. They accepted the classic liberal view that private individuals knew more and better about their needs and local conditions. But they did not claim anymore that the sum of their decisions would produce balanced or optimal outcomes. Rather, they argued, the advantage in leaving economic decisions to free markets was only visible in the very long run. Freer systems suffered from crises and periods of disequilibrium but they adapted better in the evolutionary long run. Planned economies might run more smoothly, but they were more likely to smoothly run in the wrong direction until it was too late to turn around. From this vantage point, the one thing worse than an economic slump were the attempts to avoid it.

The Olympian perspective adopted by Hayek led him to see problems of long-term economic development that economists who were concerned with the short term could easily miss. However, looking at economic questions in terms of decades or centuries, rather than quarters, also led to problems of its own. Economic historians – especially those with academic tenure – may be able to look at economic fluctuations from a perspective of intellectual curiosity. But the economic prospects and the life plans of ordinary individuals could be wrecked by what was only a minor statistical blip to an academic observer. It was for this reason that Keynes had warned policy-makers that 'the long run is a misleading guide to current affairs'.[7]

Hayek was not unaware of such problems. As his biographer Alan Ebenstein points out, he was deeply concerned about his own economic prospects for much of his life. Only when he was appointed to a chair at the University of Freiburg that entitled him to a secure state pension did this preoccupation abate. Hayek was also aware of the potential for political and social tensions that could result from individual economic insecurity. But he believed stability could be maintained if individuals understood that periods of economic austerity were inflicted not by the conscious decisions of a political or other 'man-made' authority, but by the blind and inexorable forces of the market. In his view, the failure of the austerity policies of Brüning and others was therefore mainly attributable not to the fact that they were based on erroneous economic theories, but rather to the weakness of contemporary societies and political systems. Looking back at British austerity policies of the interwar period he remarked: 'The very painful, and silly, process of deflation was very nearly successful at the end of the '20s. Then they got frightened by the long period of unemployment. I think if they had lasted a year or two longer they probably would have succeeded.'[8]

Hayek's assessment of the Great Depression also draws attention to another difficulty in his arguments. His emphasis was clearly on the long run, but he did not explain just how long that was. Looking at the arguments of classical liberal economists, it was fairly easy to see whether the predicted outcomes about the workings of self-regulating markets were accurate or not. Incidentally, the Great Depression revealed the weakness of many predictions based on classical liberal economics. The accuracy of Hayek's theory was more difficult to assess. Every crisis, no matter how long and deep, could be seen as a transitory but necessary step in the development of an economy that was, in the long run, on a superior path of development. It was not clear when the day of reckoning would come when the performances of different types of economies would be compared and when the explanatory power of Hayek's theory could also be judged.

This is not merely a problem for economists looking to test competing theories in their field. It is a problem for anyone who wants to determine which economic policies work and which do not. Thatcher's death in 2013 triggered a controversial debate about her legacy. One defining feature of the different points of view in this debate were the time frames on which commentators based their judgements. Those looking at the short-term effects of her policies were bound to be highly critical of her: Thatcher became Prime Minister in 1979 and during the first five years of her government unemployment rose from 5.3 to 11.9 per cent and growth rates were negative for most of the first two years of her premiership.

Those, in turn, who argued that the effects of her economic policies extended well into the 1990s were able to paint a much more positive picture of her achievements. Growth and employment were strong in this period and the UK outperformed comparable countries such as France economically.

However, those adopting a similar medium-term perspective often struggled to explain why the benefits of Thatcher's policies only materialised after a long delay, casting doubt on the existence of a causal link.

Finally, another set of commentators decided to judge Thatcher's economic legacy based on outcomes that manifested themselves nearly thirty years after she became Prime Minister, close to the time of her death. The excessive risk-taking of financial institutions that caused the financial crisis of 2007, they argued, was in part made possible by the deregulation of financial markets that was initiated under Thatcher. The disastrous long-term effects on the UK economy of her policies put into perspective the more positive medium-term outcomes. 'Today,' Martin Wolf, the chief economics commentator of the *Financial Times*, remarked on the day of Thatcher's death, 'the post-Thatcher renaissance looks as much illusion as reality.'[9]

However, it is important to remember that for Hayek the question of economic performance remained secondary. His main concern was that economic planning would lead to a loss of liberty. Ostensibly, government interventions were limited to economic matters and, moreover, undertaken for the benefit of individuals. However, the ultimate result of such efforts, no matter how well intended they were, would always be the loss of individual freedom and the concomitant rise of a totalitarian regime.

Planning was inevitably liberticidal because planners, in order to reach their goals, had to take important decisions out of the hands of individuals. When the state decided to put a public investment programme into place to alleviate the consequences of an economic slump, this comprised a whole string of decisions that impacted on the lives of individuals. If the programme was a construction project, planners had to decide what and where to build. By taking a decision about new infrastructures they also decided, for example, whether the comfort of drivers in Surrey was worth more than that of rail passengers in Midlothian or whether an improved water supply for the citizens of Belfast was more important than a new pedestrian bridge in London. In a similar way, the state had to set priorities when it expanded other forms of spending. Planners were forced to choose between better provision for handicapped, elderly or unemployed people. Or they might be forced to choose between healthier Scots and better educated Welsh.

At the same time, more planning also meant restrictions on the ability of individuals to take decisions about the use of their resources. In a free society, one man might decide to buy better education for his children while his neighbour might prefer to use her money for better health care. This liberty was taken away from individuals as the state took an increasing amount of decisions about the ways in which the nation's wealth was used.

It might be objected that individual freedom is not limited so long as a democratic government takes the decisions: individuals merely express their preferences collectively through the state. Hayek disagreed. Democratic institutions, he argued, were never truly in control of the state's actions. In economic planning, decisions had to be taken continuously, often at short notice and in response to changing circumstances. Democratic institutions were too slow to decide more than the general framework. Specific decisions would almost inevitably have to be taken in a more or less autocratic way, because there was no time for lengthy consultations and because the questions at hand were often too arcane to be decided by non-experts.

The undemocratic nature of economic planning was all the more perilous because it was impossible to limit it to economic matters. As Hayek pointed out, most aspects of life are in one way or another economic because they involve the use of material resources. Government control of economic matters would therefore eventually lead to totalitarian control of most aspects of life. No one summarises this problem better than Hayek himself: 'Economic control is not merely control of a sector of human life which can be separated from the rest; it is the control of the means for all of our ends. And whoever has sole control of the means must also determine which ends are to be served, which values are to be rated higher and which lower – in short, what men should believe and strive for.'[10]

The problem of a creeping loss of liberty was also a psychological one. The growing power of the state not only deprived individuals of the freedom to choose, but they were also lulled into a false sense of security. When confronted with challenges, men and women living under the benevolent dictatorship of a welfare state would cease to look to their own resources, creativity and ability. As a result, individuals would become weaker and more similar. Variety and individual ambition would eventually cease to function as driving forces for evolutionary progress. Individual liberty and its benefits for society would be irrevocably lost.

One might wonder whether individuals were not free to make a similar choice: trade in their liberty, along with any evolutionary long-term benefits that would accrue to future generations, for a little prosperity and security in the present. For Hayek, this kind of Faustian bargain was not acceptable.

Liberty, to him, was humanity's 'most precious inheritance'. The reason for this did not lie in any outcomes that freedom helped to produce. Liberty was not a means but rather 'in itself the highest political end'.[11] Why liberty rather than any other value should occupy this prominent position, Hayek did not explain.

It should be noted that for Hayek, not all types of planning were equally harmful. For example, unemployment benefits were more damaging than public works programmes because they distorted the labour market more lastingly. However, despite such subtle differences, Hayek was content to summarise his argument in a simple rule of thumb: the bigger the state, the bigger the threat to liberty. This immutable advocacy for a small state set Hayek apart from Keynes and many other economists who argued that the size of the state should fluctuate anti-cyclically to compensate for the increasing and decreasing dynamism of the private sector. For Hayek the size of the state was not a matter of economic pragmatism but of political principle. Only in certain fields that liberalism had traditionally seen as the preserves of the state such as the provision of justice and defence did Hayek consider government expenditure to be acceptable. This did not mean that the state could not be active elsewhere. As long as intervention remained limited to setting rules rather than actively planning for specific outcomes, Hayek thought state intervention acceptable and even necessary. A stable framework of predictable rules and institutions on which individuals could rely when they took decisions was crucial. As such, the most important institutions for the state to protect were private property and a stable currency. Without them, liberty became impossible and decline inevitable.

In practice, the politicians of the 1980s who claimed Hayek as a source of inspiration were not always guided by these principles, but they still emerge as principal elements of the period's reform agenda. A tight monetary policy with high interest rates was intended to ensure monetary stability. Simultaneously, government expenditure was reduced in order to ensure balanced budgets and reduce the size of the state. This maxim led to reductions in government expenditure for both investment and consumption. However, welfare spending was reduced with particular zeal because of its implications for the labour market. At the same time, defence spending often expanded, dramatically in some countries, in order to defend free societies against external threats. In addition, measures were taken to limit government regulation and allow the forces of competition to work more fully: the most important of these measures were the attempts to limit the influence of trade unions in the labour market. The result was that the late 1970s and early 1980s became periods of economic hardship for large numbers in many Western countries.

'There is little or no economic theory in the book'

Hayek proposed powerful arguments that shaped the intellectual climate and economic development of more than one country. However, despite their great influence on economic policy, Hayek's arguments were mainly based on political and philosophical considerations. He acknowledged as much in the introduction to *The Road to Serfdom*, where he called it a 'political book'.[12] Many of Hayek's readers agreed. When Hayek submitted the manuscript of *The Road to Serfdom* for publication, Chicago University Press asked the economist Frank

Knight (1885–1972) for a reader's report. Knight, the founding father of the 'Chicago school' of economics, was sympathetic to Hayek's opinions, but critical of the manuscript. 'There is little or no economic theory in the book,' he noted. He also expressed doubts about the 'desirability of publishing this book' in the United States.[13] This prompted the editor to ask for a second opinion from another reader. In the event, the second opinion was more positive. Hayek encountered this ambiguous mixture of admiration and doubts about his credentials as an economist more than once in his career. At the LSE, he had taught in the economics department, but when he put himself forward for a position at the University of Chicago the economics department refused to hire him. He was instead appointed at the university's interdisciplinary Committee on Social Thought. One of the most prominent members of the economics department in Chicago, Friedman, later observed, 'I am an enormous admirer of Hayek, but not for his economics.'[14]

The ambiguous attitudes of many economists to Hayek's work was unsurprising given the nature of the questions he was considering. Issues of economic outcomes or economic efficiency, which are the mainstay of professional economists, were secondary to him. He was mainly concerned with the protection of certain values, above all liberty, and the question of which political structures were conducive to this end. He certainly had views on specific questions of economic theory, but they were neither particularly innovative nor were they his most pressing concerns. In contrast with traditional liberalism, Hayek's neoliberalism places him in a long tradition of thinkers – some of whom are included in this book – who approached economic life from an essentially non-economic perspective.

Misunderstood and ignored

Despite the fact that there was 'little or no economic theory' in Hayek's book, it still presented powerful arguments. At least this is how many have come to think of *The Road to Serfdom* in retrospect. Contemporaries were much less impressed with the book. Initial sales were not as bad as Knight had predicted, but Hayek's work was neither a great commercial success nor was it particularly influential in the intellectual and political debates of the post-war decades.

The reason for the lukewarm reception may lie in the contrast between Hayek's predictions and the experience of most of his readers. During the war virtually all Western economies had become planned economies. The post-war period did not bring fundamental change in this respect. Certain forms of planning such as rationing came to an end, but welfare provisions expanded rapidly after the war and monetary and fiscal policy were systematically used to ensure full employment. Hayek had warned that the expansion of planning would be the prelude to a loss of liberty, but many in the Western world had a different experience in this period: by the early 1970s, women had acquired greater freedom than ever before in most Western countries. In the same period, African Americans began to harvest the fruits of their long struggle for civil rights.

There can be no question that repression was also part of the history of this period. The 1950s were the period of Senator McCarthy's anti-Communist witch-hunts in the US, and protests against the Vietnam War were often violently repressed in the 1960s and 1970s. In Europe, the student movement of the late 1960s and the subsequent wave of left-wing terrorism provoked violent and oppressive reactions from governments. Nonetheless, on the whole, these were decades of growing, not diminishing individual freedom. Hayek rightly pointed out that fascist and democratic governments alike increasingly used economic planning from the early 1930s. But despite these similarities in economic policy, the development of political conditions was radically different. It became clear in this period that forms of economic planning were equally compatible with the Nuremberg laws of Nazi Germany and the Civil Rights Act of contemporary America.

Seen in the very long run the nexus between the size of the state and individual freedom seems even more tenuous. Arguments similar to those of Hayek had first been propounded by the Prussian liberal Wilhelm von Humboldt (1767–1835) in his tract *The Limits of State Action* of 1791–2. Obviously, Humboldt was not concerned with the implications of Keynesian planning. He was worried about the excessive political and economic power of the state in his period. Absolutist states in the mould of his native Prussia and contemporary republican states such as France had far-reaching ambitions to ensure the welfare of their citizens in economic and other respects. According to Humboldt, this kind of governmental paternalism was extremely harmful for the development of individuals and societies. Like Hayek, he advocated the tightest possible limits on state action to allow individuals and societies to evolve freely.

With hindsight his warnings seem exaggerated. The size of government has increased vastly since Humboldt's time but it is not easy to mount a convincing case that inhabitants of Berlin or other formerly Prussian territories that are today part of Germany are less free now than they were in 1792. Those who were serfs in the Prussian villages at the time would probably find it hard to make sense of the notion that today's inhabitants of rural Brandenburg find themselves on a road to serfdom due to the extent of welfare provisions that they are entitled to. Similarly, freedom of expression was greater in Berlin in 1792 than in most other places at the time, but urban dwellers in Germany today enjoy far greater civil liberties despite the greater size of the state.

Historical experience has largely discredited simple arguments about an inverse correlation between the state's size and individual liberty. Nonetheless, it would be rash to dismiss the arguments of Humboldt and Hayek wholesale. From what we know today about developmental psychology, it is clear that exposure to a wide variety of experiences from an early age is fundamental for individual development. Equally important is the freedom to choose careers and leisure pursuits that mesh with individual talents and preferences. Individuals who are deprived of this liberty grow up without fully developing their capacities and may suffer psychologically.

The radical individualism of Humboldt and Hayek anticipated such arguments. But they rushed to conclusions when they identified the expansion of the state as the sole or even principal threat to individual liberty. In practice, the ability of children and other individuals to make their own choices and be exposed to varied experiences may be limited by a whole variety of factors. Oppressive family structures and the workings of free markets can be as limiting as the regulations of an overbearing state. State-led systems of education often constrain individual development when governments seek to channel individuals into professions that will be needed in the future or when government ministers seek to shape school and university curricula for the presumed economic needs of tomorrow. But private systems of education can equally prevent individuals from fully developing their abilities when access to education depends on wealth rather than on talent.

Since the times of Humboldt and Hayek, it has become clear that the experiences of individuals within modern states have varied widely. When answering the question of whether states are enemies or allies of individual liberty, attention has therefore shifted away from the question of the state's size. Instead, we need to examine every state individually and ask what its aims and objectives are and what power relations it embodies.

Finally shaping the world

There remains the question of how *The Road to Serfdom* went from being the largely ignored publication of a largely ignored Austrian professor to becoming the manual of one of the greatest revolutions in economic policy of the twentieth century. Quite apart from the loose ends in Hayek's arguments, timing suggests that the power of his ideas was not the sole factor in this success story. The book was published in the 1940s but the neoliberal revolutions took place only in the 1970s and 1980s.

If we look more closely at the historical context, it emerges that, paradoxically, the successes of Keynesian economic policies were the main causes for the triumph of Hayek's teachings: true to its promise, Keynesianism had produced high and stable growth along with low unemployment in the post-war decades. Between 1951 and 1973 average global growth was 4.8 per cent. Average unemployment in Germany in this period was 3.1 per cent, 1.6 in the UK and 1.2 in France. The protracted economic boom earned the period the nickname of the 'golden age of capitalism'. But in truly dialectical fashion, this success also produced economic and political outcomes that eventually led to the end of Keynesian policies.

It is often said that the 'stagflation' of the early 1970s led to the defeat of Keynesianism. According to this argument, Keynesian analysis could not explain the combination of stagnating economic growth and high inflation that occurred in many Western economies in this period. In the eyes of many contemporaries, 'stagflation' thus delivered a deadly double blow: it was evidence that Keynesian economic policies could not ensure economic prosperity in the long run and, at the same time, it discredited the theoretical foundations on which these policies rested.

With hindsight, the effects of 'stagflation' appear simpler. Keynesian economic policies were discredited by the fact that they ceased to produce prosperity. However, the added notion that 'stagflation' was inexplicable in Keynesian terms seems misleading. On the contrary, the Keynesian 'paradox of thrift' offers a simple and compelling explanation of what went wrong in the period.

The low unemployment rates of the post-war period along with generous welfare provisions for the unemployed meant that unions were in a singularly strong bargaining position. Over the years this led to substantial wage increases. This boosted consumer demand but it also meant that the problem of excessive saving reappeared. As Keynes and others had pointed out, the savings rate increased with income. In other words, those with higher incomes tended to save a greater proportion of their income than low-income earners. As more households earned more, they also saved more. However, in order to maintain full employment, investments had to match savings. This became increasingly difficult because of the sustained and prolonged increase in savings. Ever greater volumes of investment were necessary to secure growth.

For a number of reasons, investment failed to keep up with saving in this period. In part, this was due to the simple fact that investment opportunities depend to a substantial extent on the random progress of technology. Whether profitable investments can be made and how much capital is required depend largely on the nature of recent innovation: compared with the size of the economy the cost of building railway networks in the nineteenth century was simply much higher than were the costs of putting a computer on every office desk in the last decades of the twentieth century. Keynesianism might have been saved by the invention of costly new technology in the early 1970s. However, none was forthcoming. On the contrary, the oil shocks of the period with their spikes in oil prices dented the prospects of some of the principal industries, including the automotive industry.

Another factor posed an even more important obstacle to sufficient investment. The strong growth in wages made investments less appealing. Since wage increases frequently outpaced productivity growth in the 'golden decades', wages grew at the expense of profits in many sectors. The rate of return on investments decreased. This did not mean that there were no profitable investment opportunities anymore, but profit rates were squeezed by wage increases.

One might assume that investments would be made as long as *any* profit was to be expected. However, as Keynes had argued, investment decisions were not necessarily rational. The expectations of investors played a crucial role. If the rate of profit that investors were likely to realise fell below the return which they considered acceptable they would not part with their money at all, or would seek other, more profitable placements elsewhere. In the 1970s a similar situation caused an 'investors' strike' that resulted in slow growth and falling employment. At the same time, the failure to invest limited the increase in productive capacity. Since demand remained strong, inflation resulted.

Was it inevitable that this cocktail of stagnation and inflation became the cup of hemlock for Keynesianism? In the 1930s Keynes had predicted that a time would come when the state would have to take investment decisions out of the hands of private individuals. It can be argued that this moment had arrived in the 1970s. Sufficient investment could only be maintained if governments were prepared to force investors to content themselves with lower profit rates. This would not necessarily have meant expropriating them or depriving them of profits altogether. But it would have meant extending planning even further.

The reasons that this route was not taken were more political than economic. Among the mainstream left in most European countries there was little appetite to expand the government's role in the economy. At this time, the prospect of becoming more similar to the planned economies of the communist countries had lost much of its appeal. Largely as a result of Keynesian policies, capitalism seemed to most working men and women to be a more attractive option than the command economies of the East.

Unsurprisingly, there was even less sympathy for additional planning among employers and on the right of the political spectrum. By the early 1970s, a growing number of wealthy individuals, entrepreneurs, professionals and executives had grown tired of high tax rates and a political climate in which the odds were consistently stacked against them. Not unlike the employer associations of the Weimar Republic, many believed that it was time to get out of a political consensus that they, or their predecessors, had accepted mainly because it seemed the lesser evil at the time. When Keynesianism became the new consensus in the 1930s, the apparent alternative was the collapse of capitalism. This was in some respects similar to the circumstance under which Weimar employers had entered the Stinnes–Legien agreement in 1918. After the threat of political and economic collapse had abated, the necessities imposed by the Second World War and its preparation prevented a resurgence of economic individualism. Part of the war effort was a heightened sense of national unity. This sentiment persisted after the war and made it difficult to openly oppose welfare provisions and other forms of planning; in particular, because the main beneficiaries were often those who had fought in the war or made great sacrifices for the defence of the nation.

However, with the passing of time, memories of the Great Depression and the Second World War faded. Moreover, decades of state interference and ever increasing union power felt like a Via Dolorosa to many employers and convinced many that it was time to stem the political tide. Wealthy donors were increasingly prepared to spend substantial amounts of money on disseminating alternative views to Keynesianism. The Volker Fund, a private charity founded by a self-made entrepreneur who had earned a fortune in home furnishings, partly funded Hayek's appointment at Chicago. The original purpose of the charity had been to help the needy, but by this time the founder's nephew had expanded the activities of the fund into promoting free market ideas. Similarly, the first meeting of Hayek's Mont Pelerin Society of neoliberal thinkers was financed by Swiss bankers and business people, as well as American foundations, including the Volker Fund. Libertarian think tanks such as the Cato Institute and the Reason Foundation that still play an important role in shaping public debates today were founded in this period. Much of the success of these think tanks is due to their substantial resources and their disciplined and well-focused work. Nonetheless, like the efforts of Foster and Catchings a few decades earlier, it is unlikely that their work would have had the same success had it not taken place in the context of a deep economic crisis.

A new age

As a result of the economic crisis and concomitant political shifts, Hayek's views exercised a strong influence on policy-makers and the wider public. This paradigm shift in the late twentieth century is particularly important because in many respects it shaped the economic and intellectual context in which we confront the present economic crisis. Periods of austerity were central to Hayek's vision: in his view, a small state was always desirable, but in particular in times of crisis governments had to show restraint and abstain from additional consumption and investment. If government did not behave virtuously in such periods and instead sought an easy solution to economic woes by expanding spending, this would harm recovery and long-term prospects. Private individuals, too, needed to exercise restraint. Only sufficient saving could lay the foundations for renewed investment. The state's task was to support the efforts of savers by preventing inflation. In addition to calling for restraint on the part of private individuals and states, Hayek's best advice was to trust the dynamism of a free society and let any crisis run its course.

In the 1930s his advice was ultimately not heard, but in the late 1970s he had the ear of those in power in the UK and elsewhere. The consequence was a set of policy measures that aggravated the economic downturn. But unlike earlier versions of liberal arguments Hayek's neoliberalism was not damaged by the worsening economic performance. He never promised a rose garden: the economic suffering resulting from the crisis was expected and inevitable. It was the price to pay for liberty. Short-term fluctuations in GDP or employment were simply irrelevant in this context. Higher values were at stake.

It is perhaps no coincidence that Thatcher used religious language to characterise the nature of her convictions: 'The Old Testament prophets did not say, "Brothers, I want a consensus." They said, "This is my faith. This is what I passionately believe. If you believe it too, then come with me." '[15] Thatcher saw herself as on a mission to bring a revealed truth to the world and fight for its triumph. This admirable force of conviction helped her to win many political battles but it left little space for second thoughts and critical examination of the practical outcomes produced by her crusade.

Despite winning the Nobel Prize for economics, Hayek's most important and lasting achievement may well not lie in his contribution to that discipline. Rather he stands out as the thinker who convinced political leaders, and with them large parts of the broader public, that economic policy decisions should not be based primarily on the economic outcomes which they produce in the short and medium term. This repudiation of economic pragmatism places Hayek in an intellectual tradition that is closer to the pre-modern thinkers who wrote before Mandeville than to many of the later commentators who shared a commitment to economic efficiency as the principal yardstick by which to measure the success or failure of economic policies.

CHAPTER 7

Austerity for the planet
green ideas of consumption

In the same decade as Hayek's ideas gained popularity, an entirely different type of consumption critique was also gaining prominence. While neoliberals warned that liberty would be lost if states did not tighten their belts, ecologists claimed that the survival of the entire planet depended on everyone – individuals, companies and states – cutting down on consumption. Ideas about the protection of the environment have a long tradition in Western culture and elsewhere, but the publication of a small book entitled *The Limits to Growth* in 1972 marked a watershed in public debates about the topic.

Since the 1970s, green thought has greatly expanded its influence on politics. In the West, it is now one of the principal currents of political thought. And while the green movement has many factions, it is clear that abstinence from consumption is a central concern shared by virtually all of them. Without changing how much and what we consume, most people with environmental concerns agree, humanity is doomed.

Perhaps more emphatically than the other critics of consumption discussed here, greens reject the economic perspective on consumption. Faced with the threat of man-made apocalypse, the economic implications of abstinence inevitably become a trivial concern. Who could possibly worry about what an increase or decline in consumption does to economic growth or unemployment when survival is at stake. Most traditions of green thought also agree that technological fixes, or a mere fine-tuning of the current system, are not sufficient to save the planet. Such measures can only prolong nature's agony, they cannot stop it. Greens call for humanity to radically change its ways and adopt new ethics that include the virtues of moderation, restraint and abstinence. Levels of consumption need to be set not with the aim of maximising economic efficiency, but so that they conform with the ethical imperatives of protecting the survival of humankind and nature. In this sense, green thought inserts itself into an intellectual tradition that seeks to set a level of consumption that is 'just', but that may be quite different from the level required for economies to run at full capacity.

Green ideas already had a long history when they came on the political scene in a forceful way from the 1970s. This chapter first explores the historical traditions on which green ideas build and then concentrates on their current form. Needless to say, green thought is only explored to the extent that is necessary to understand the green perspectives on consumption. This intellectual tradition has more to offer but it would be impossible, as well as distracting, to attempt a comprehensive discussion here.

The deep roots of green

The notion that misguided patterns of consumption can bring about the end of the world, or at least of a community, is not new. The story of Sodom and Gomorrah, for example, forms a central part of the Judeo-Christian religious tradition. For centuries similar religious and mythical visions of apocalypse have helped to impress the message of abstinence and moderation on Western populations.

However, the notion that excessive consumption could trigger apocalypse remained influential even as Western culture evolved from one based primarily on religious foundations to one made in the mould of the Enlightenment. In 1797, Malthus described how the unfettered sexual appetites of mankind would lead to a dramatic rise in population numbers. The resulting increase in consumption of food and other material goods would eventually exceed the planet's productive capacity and nature would re-establish what we might today call a 'sustainable' level of consumption by brutal means. Thousands would starve to death. However, since sexual appetites were unlikely to abate, constant population pressure would prevent the mass of the population from rising above subsistence level. No matter how much progress could be made in the production of food or other commodities, population growth would always be faster. The result was that the majority of mankind was doomed to live a precarious existence at subsistence level.

Although Malthus was a cleric, his predictions did not rely on the intervention of a punishing God. The power of arithmetic, along with certain assumptions about human nature, was at the centre of his theory. The crux was that most men and women were unable to control their sex drives. In the absence of effective contraception this would inevitably lead to high birth rates.

Only a small part of society was able to resist sexual urges effectively and limit the number of their offspring through abstinence. These were outstanding individuals who combined two qualities. First, they had sufficient foresight to understand that a limited number of children would be better for the welfare of their families as well as for the future prospects of their children. Second, these superior individuals commanded exceptional moral strength that enabled them to put their rational understanding into practice and resist their primitive appetites. In short, such superior individuals were able to forgo present carnal pleasure for future economic rewards for themselves and their children. There is an uncanny similarity to the characteristics which Smith and Weber ascribed to the men and women who were able to accumulate capital and thus emerge from the mass of the propertyless proletariat. Smith and Weber had described the middle class as the milieu best suited for abstinence from consumption. Perhaps unsurprisingly, Malthus identified the same class as the one best suited to the practice of sexual abstinence.

Alas, only a small share of the population was intellectually and morally equipped to become frigid entrepreneurs. The remaining majority was composed of promiscuous proletarians. They produced numerous offspring who were bound subsequently to adopt the sexual patterns typical of their class. The result was *exponential* population growth and a corresponding increase in the consumption of food and other material resources. However, because of the limitation of arable land, food production did not increase at the same speed and would eventually stagnate.

The simplicity and elegance of Malthus's argument remain captivating. However, perhaps even more fascinating is how misguided Malthus's predictions seem in retrospect. He predicted widespread and inevitable misery for the majority of populations. Clearly, such fears were not borne out by actual developments in the Western world. Enormous inequalities persist and poverty is a reality even in the industrialised world, but hardly anyone in Western Europe or North America lives in the kind of misery predicted by Malthus. Instead, virtually everybody today lives better than most of Malthus's contemporaries. The vast majority of Westerners live very comfortable lives and a substantial margin separates their level of consumption from anything that could be defined as poverty.

The historical outcomes differed from Malthus's predictions mainly because populations did not grow as expected. From the last quarter of the nineteenth century, birth rates declined, sometimes dramatically, in many parts of Europe. The demographic long-term trends in Europe remained far below the feared exponential growth. In part, the causes were cultural and social changes. More people developed the kind of foresight and aspirations that Malthus had seen as the preserve of the middle class. At the same time, the shift from agrarian to industrialised societies meant that in many families children were no longer cheap additional farmhands. Additional children were often no longer an economic advantage but, rather, a burden.

However, many historical demographers believe that the single most important blow was dealt to Malthus's theory by the inventors Charles Goodyear and Thomas Hancock. The later registered a UK patent for the process of rubber vulcanisation in 1844, while the former obtained a US patent for the same process in 1847. Among the uses to which the new technology was put was the production of cheaper and more reliable condoms. The inventions of other chemists equally left their mark on demographic patterns: in the early twentieth century the latex condom was invented, and from 1960 contraceptive pills became available in most Western countries. The sum of these inventions meant that men and women could give in to their sexual desires without causing exponential population growth. The new situation in which it became possible to 'have one's cake and eat it' was morally suspect to many. But there can be no doubt that technology had found a simple and elegant solution to a seemingly inescapable existential threat faced by humanity.

Despite their shortcomings Malthus's theories have remained a source of inspiration for social scientists and environmentalists. One may see in Malthus the forbear of the anthropocentric tradition in green thought. This is the notion that the environment is worth saving because, and to the extent that, the survival of humanity depends on it. In particular, the perils for humanity's survival associated with forms of exponential growth that Malthus discussed have remained a main concern in green thought today. Much of it centres on the view that – if left unchecked – increasing resource consumption, driven by exponentially growing populations, industrial production and other parameters, could create extremely adverse living conditions on earth.

Another of Malthus's concerns that has remained important for the development of green thought was the notion that only a small part of the population possesses the foresight, altruism and moral fortitude required not to consummate or consume in the present in order to secure future gain and, in particular, to protect the welfare of future generations. Similar views remain important in today's green movements. They have contributed to associating green thought with connotations of moral superiority and have led many green activists to develop a significant educational zeal.

This perspective is not without importance to the theoretical tenets of green thought as well. Important strands of green thought advocate authoritarian measures to curb consumption and other 'un-green' behaviour. In part, such interference with individual freedom is justified by reference to the lack of moral maturity and excessive egoism of the multitude. In this view, the limited knowledge and ethical awareness displayed by most men and women today make it impossible to rely on the individual sense of responsibility to do what is necessary for survival.

The early nineteenth century also produced another intellectual tradition that contributed much to the development of modern green thought: Romanticism. As increasing parts of Europe's nature were consumed by rapid industrial growth and urbanisation, artists, writers and intellectuals began to question modernity. The search for alternatives to the cold rationality of the industrial age led many to adopt new perspectives on nature. Romantic critics blamed the Enlightenment for looking at nature as a mere accumulation of inert matter that existed primarily to be dominated, transformed, used and consumed by mankind. In contrast, Romanticism proposed a more emotional and holistic approach. Nature was seen as a source of edification that had the power to inspire humanity morally and artistically. Nature was also seen to have an intrinsic value, quite separate from the use that humanity could make of it.

Romantics were wary of damaging nature because of the adverse effects that this could have on humanity. Characteristic is Mary Wollstonecraft Shelley's early nineteenth-century story about the disastrous results yielded by the scientific efforts of Dr Victor Frankenstein. The ambitious doctor made a creature that eventually turned against him and his loved ones. The analogy is simple and forceful: armed with science and industry, humanity was now able to provoke developments that could escape its control and pose a serious threat to human existence. However, significantly Shelley's allegorical novel warns not only of the negative implications of progress for humanity; the suffering of Frankenstein's creature is as much part of the damage done by the 'modern Prometheus' as is the suffering of the human characters in the novel. Shelley's concern was with humanity harming itself, but it was equally about the suffering of nature in its own right.[1]

Some of the more radical parts of modern green thought are influenced by the ethical tradition that developed out of Romanticism. In this view, humans must respect nature because its creatures and natural habitats as a whole have a right to be protected. This right does not spring from the use value that nature represents for humans. Rather nature has the right to remain unscathed in the same way as humans enjoy certain inalienable rights simply by virtue of existing. Similar views mark a radical departure from many strands of Western ethics, which ascribe rights and duties mostly to humans. The Judeo-Christian tradition, for example, knows a duty of care by mankind to nature. However, this duty does not flow from the intrinsic rights of nature, but is a part of the covenant between God and humanity: the imperative to respect nature results from the respect for God and the commitments that humanity made to Him.

Different types of green thought may lead to different perspectives on consumption: seen from a 'light green' anthropocentric perspective, the question of whether or not to eat

meat, or a certain type of fish, or the question of what material to use for a new shelf can be answered by gauging the
impact that this may have on the survival of the planet. From
a 'deep green' perspective, the individual rights of the animals
and plants involved ought to be valued and balanced against
human needs.

The different attitudes towards consumption of 'light' and
'deep' green traditions are well illustrated by a thought exper-
iment proposed by the environmental philosopher Robin
Attfield. Think of a situation in which the last surviving human
after a nuclear holocaust has to decide whether or not he
should cut down a tree in order to use it for firewood. Would
this man be doing anything wrong in cutting down the tree,
knowing that he would die before the tree if he left the tree
alone? For those of a 'light green' persuasion, the answer is
clear: since no negative impact is to be feared on the chances of
survival of humanity (in this case numbering one), it is perfectly
acceptable to cut down the tree. However, if one accepts that
the tree has an intrinsic right to live, then things become more
complicated. Arboreal rights and human needs have to be
weighed against each other. A cold last supper for the last
surviving human would be a likely outcome of this ethical
dilemma.

Shades of green

Different traditions of green thought rest on fundamentally
different theoretical foundations, but in practice their positions
with regard to consumption often converge. For one, the
different shades of green share a common passion for submitting
themselves and others to a punishing regime of abstinence from

consumption. Both currents advocate abstinence from consumption even in circumstances where this may hurt the economic welfare of humans and where discomfort and even suffering may be the result. Or, in the words of the environmentalist George Monbiot: 'The campaign against climate change is ... not for abundance but for austerity. It is a campaign not for more freedom but for less. Strangest of all it is a campaign not just against other people, but also against ourselves.'[2] It could almost seem that one of the sources of satisfaction in adopting green convictions lies in the deprivation, material and otherwise, which greens bring on themselves and others. In fact, abstinence is often not merely practised but celebrated. Turning Veblen on his head, we encounter today individuals practising 'ostentatious abstinence': politicians swapping limousines for bicycles are only the most visible manifestation of this phenomenon.

The theoretical foundations on which different green convictions rest often matter little in practice. Light greens may ask you to switch from your habitual steak dinner to having tofu stir-fry because the amount of resources consumed and the emissions produced in raising cattle endanger the planet. Deep greens, in contrast, will ask you to switch to plant feed in order to protect the animal rights of cattle. No matter how different these approaches are in theory, the practical implications are similar. Moreover, both approaches agree that the resulting economic decline of cattle-farming areas and the lost economic growth are irrelevant in the face of pressing environmental concerns.

In both perspectives, light and deep green, ethical concerns trump short-term considerations about economic efficiency. Crucially, both traditions also agree in placing altruism above selfish concerns. For light greens, the rights and welfare of

future generations are paramount and will often take prece-
dence over concerns with the present. For dark greens, the
rights and welfare of animals and other organisms matter in the
same way. In both paradigms, humans are called upon by
ethical imperatives to consider not only their own interests but
also those of individuals and organisms that do not have a
voice in the political process because they have not yet been
born, or because they cannot speak.

The Limits to Growth

The heterogeneous traditions that inform green thought and
the wide popularity of green ideas make it extremely difficult
to answer the question of what a green perspective on consumption looks like today. No single leader or organisation represents the green movement. Nonetheless, there are some texts
that are regarded as fundamental by most greens and that mark
the rise of the modern green movement. Among those texts,
The Limits to Growth occupies a prominent position. The book
'is hard to beat as a symbol for the birth of ecologism in its fully
contemporary guise', writes Andrew Dobson, a leading theorist
of green thought.[3]

The small book was published in 1972 as a report to the
Club of Rome, a think tank that had been founded only four
years earlier with the aim of exploring future challenges faced
by humanity. Funded by the Volkswagen Foundation, the
report was first presented at the St Gallen Symposium in
Switzerland. Since that time, over 12 million copies have been
sold, not counting the numerous updates and additions that
have subsequently appeared. In no small way, this book has
shaped the way greens and the wider public think about the

future of the planet in general and, more specifically, about the future of consumption.

The language of *The Limits to Growth* has none of the colour of more traditional apocalyptic accounts, but its conclusions still make for chilling reading:

> If present growth trends in world population, industrializa-
> tion, pollution, food production, and resource depletion
> continue unchanged, the limits to growth on this planet will
> be reached sometime within the next hundred years. The
> most probable result will be a rather sudden and uncontrol-
> lable decline in both population and industrial capacity.[4]

Lest readers should entertain futile hopes, the report specifies that the final decline will be caused by an abrupt increase in the death rate caused by pollution and starvation.

The predicted outcomes have a distinctly Malthusian flavour, and the mechanisms that drive the development are also partly familiar. The central problem identified in *The Limits to Growth* is once again exponential growth. In particular, exponential population and industrial growth are seen as critical. They are not in themselves harmful. However, the increasing ability to produce commodities combined with a rapidly increasing number of consumers results in a dramatic overall increase in consumption of material goods, which in turn is responsible for making the planet unliveable.

In this scenario, mounting consumption of physical goods leads to rapid depletion of limited natural resources such as oil and metal ores. As resources become scarcer, the cost of extraction rises and ever greater amounts of capital need to be devoted to this end. (In a recent book, *2052: A Global Forecast for*

the Next Forty Years, Jørgen Randers, one of the original authors
of *The Limits to Growth*, discusses a variant of this mechanism:
in this view ever higher levels of investment become necessary
to compensate for the effects of climate change, and this saps
capital from productive use.) As less capital can be devoted to
production, industrial output declines. Since agricultural
production has become highly dependent on industrial products such as fertilisers and machinery (today one could add
genetically modified seeds), food production collapses along
with industrial output. Industrial decline also limits the ability
to provide medical care because of its reliance on industrially
produced pharmaceuticals and equipment. As food production
and medical care are reduced, mortality escalates, pushing
down population numbers and consumption.

Two factors cause this final process to be apocalyptic rather
than gradual. First, exponential growth is extremely fast and
therefore 'deceptive'.[5] It may be enough to 'blink once' in order
to miss the passing of a critical threshold. Second, the effects of
positive feedback loops aggravate this risk. Population growth,
for example, will continue even after birth rates have started to
decline and pollutants may continue to cause more damage
even after their emission has been stopped. This means that
even if humanity acts as soon as the damage caused by certain
forms of growth becomes apparent, it may already be too late
to save the planet. 'Overshoot' is the term which the authors
use for this treacherous phenomenon.

Survival

The alternative to death by overshoot is a reduction in population and industrial growth. If they cease, consumption can be

stabilised and survival becomes possible in what the authors call the 'state of global equilibrium'.[6] There is, however, no detailed discussion in *The Limits to Growth* of how such a transition might be brought about. With regard to population growth, the green literature offers a range of solutions. On the more radical end of the spectrum, environmentalists have been known to describe AIDS as a disease that might save the planet by ending industrialism and population growth. More humanely minded greens advocate birth control schemes that are based on persuasion, easy access to contraceptives and sexual abstinence. Between these extremes many different solutions have been proposed that usually include more or less authoritarian interference with individual decisions about procreation.

Besides population growth, industrial expansion needs to be curbed. Increasing abstinence from consumption is usually seen as a crucial part of any attempt to reduce industrial activity. However, as the authors of *The Limits to Growth* point out, any economic activity that does not 'require a large flow of irreplaceable resources or produce severe environmental degradation might continue indefinitely'.[7] The authors imagine a stationary state, not dissimilar from that foreseen by Keynes. Humanity would learn to find fulfilment in the 'consumption' of arts, education and leisure. The acquisition of material wealth would no longer be a priority of individuals and a mark of distinction in society. Progress in productivity would be turned into greater leisure time for workers, instead of being used for additional production. Keynes's vision of a three-hour working day is, in this view, part of the solution that could save the planet.

Still, even if humanity could be brought to adopt such bohemian ways, the authors of *The Limits to Growth* expect conflicts over distribution. In the absence of industrial growth, the available material production would have to be distributed more evenly than is currently the case in order to avoid severe shortages for some. Therefore, inhabitants of the industrialised world would have to learn to value a subscription to the next season of an experimental theatre company more than a new smartphone. However, they would not only have to renounce increases in material consumption, they would also have to contend with a decreased level of material consumption. While those in the developing world might see gains in their material consumption in the equilibrium state, that state would almost certainly be associated with material deprivation for Westerners.

According to many greens, the choice for the inhabitants of industrialised nations is therefore between austerity and apocalypse. There is no third way that could offer a painless alternative because technical fixes that may save the planet while maintaining high levels of material comfort are seen to be ineffective. The main reason for this lies in the exponential nature of growth. The speed of growth means that any reduction in resource depletion and pollution that can be achieved as a result of technical innovation will be a mere drop in the ocean. The authors of *The Limits to Growth* were categorical: innovation may prolong the period of industrial and population growth, but it cannot 'remove the ultimate limits to that growth'.[8]

Most greens therefore agree that 'the changes that need to take place are too profound to be dealt with solely in the political arena, and that the psyche is as important as the parliamentary chamber'.[9] Nothing less than a new man is required. To this end some green advocates recommend the use of 'psychotechnologies'[10] in order to create 'calmer, gentler and more "green" states of consciousness'.[11]

Critics of green

One of the central problems with green thought is that many of the predictions about the apocalyptic consequences of consumption have not come true. In their 1974 book *The End of Affluence* the environmentalists Paul Ehrlich and Anne Ehrlich warned that Western societies were 'entrapped in their own unnatural love for growing gross national product'. As a consequence, they predicted that

> before 1985 mankind will enter a genuine age of scarcity in which many things besides energy will be in short supply ... Such diverse commodities as food, fresh water, copper, and paper will become increasingly difficult to obtain and thus much more expensive ... Starvation among people will be accompanied by starvation of industries for the materials they require.[12]

The Limits to Growth contained some predictions that were equally far off the mark: global reserves of gold, silver and mercury were predicted to run out in the 1980s.

Defenders of green austerity will hardly be dissuaded by similar errors. They may concede that doomsayers occasionally get the timing of apocalypse wrong. But in their view the inexorable logic of exponential growth must eventually lead to a level of consumption that exceeds the 'carrying capacity' of the planet. Critics argue that this concentration on deductive reasoning is the main problem of green thought. Many doomsday scenarios focus on what *must* happen but entirely disregard what *has* happened over the past centuries.

In his book *The Skeptical Environmentalist*, first published in 1998, the statistician Bjørn Lomborg assembles a substantial body of historical environmental data and offers a detailed critique of green thought. He warns that the models that underpin green doomsday scenarios often 'pass off a temporary truism as an important indicator of decline'.[13] This applies, for example, to the warnings about the scarcity of land and the associated limitations on food production. Since the times of Malthus, greens have warned that as population grows the limited area of arable land will be divided among an increasing number of individuals, leading to increasingly small, and eventually insufficient plots being available to feed each individual.

Lomborg points to two fundamental problems with such predictions: greens pay too little attention to empirical detail and historical evidence. With regard to the allegedly inevitable shortage of arable land, for example, they rarely bother to establish what the smallest plot size is that would still provide sufficient food to sustain one person. From the perspective of green doomsayers, this is a secondary issue. As long as a minimum plot size exists and population growth is exponential, famine can be postponed but not avoided.

Seen from this Olympian perspective it may be legitimate to disregard empirical detail. But seen from a more practical perspective, details matter. As Lomborg explains, the progress of modern agricultural technology means that today the area needed to feed one human is a mere 36 square metres. For energy production, it would be enough to cover a small part of the Sahara Desert with solar panels in order to provide for the total global consumption of energy: a mere 2.6 per cent would suffice. Such details become relevant once doubts are raised about the assumption of exponential population growth itself.

As Lomborg and others point out, birth rates have historically tended to decline with economic development and exponential population growth may well not happen as predicted.

If we accept similar criticism, this sheds a new light on the possibility of technical fixes to solve environmental problems. In fact, it is a central argument of critics that historically humanity has been successful at solving its environmental problems through technology and political and social change. Looking at long-term averages, most measures available indicate that the human condition has improved. There is little evidence of progressing resource depletion or dramatically worsening pollution. Even the problem of climate change, critics like Lomborg contend, can be successfully managed, and without bringing civilisation as we know it to a halt.

The historical evidence undercuts a crucial element of green thought. If technical fixes have been successful in the past and appear possible today, then there is no need for radical ethical change. The alternative is no longer between a new austere society and apocalypse. A less radical middle way becomes possible in which comforts and many forms of consumption can be preserved along with the planet. One of the central contentions of Lomborg is that historical data suggest that there is no trade-off between economic development and protection of the environment. 'We can forget about our fear of imminent breakdown,' he concludes. 'We can see that the world is basically headed in the right direction and that we can help to steer this development process by focusing on and insisting on reasonable prioritization.'[14]

A green reply to similar criticism is likely to refer to the concept of 'overshoot': historical development may have been largely benign up to now but, without noticing it, we have already passed a turning point after which further expansion of consumption will cause severe environmental damage. Since the consequences will only become fully apparent in the future, we cannot rely on empirical data but must trust models based on deductive reasoning. Because of feedback loops and self-reinforcing developments, humanity may very well pass the point of no return if we wait for empirical evidence that conclusively proves the existence of an imminent existential threat to the planet. Therefore, arguments for green austerity, like many other arguments for abstinence from consumption, rest to an important extent on accepting an article of faith that is not easily verifiable empirically.

If critics are right about the weak empirical foundations of green doomsday scenarios, they have to answer the question of why such apocalyptic visions are still widely accepted. Lomborg discusses several mechanisms that, according to him, limit the critical scrutiny that is applied to what he calls 'the litany': unfounded claims about environmental decline that have become part of conventional wisdom.[15]

One crucial problem relates to the disconnection between research and public debates. Research about environmental problems is usually professional, scientifically sound and cautious in its conclusions. Yet public claims derived from this research are often sensational, overblown, and taken out of context. Selective and distorting reporting in the media is partly to blame. Dramatic claims about the end of the world are bound to capture the attention of readers and viewers more than reports explaining complex developments or, indeed, news dispatches reporting that things are fine. Moreover, news about dangers to the environment is largely uncontroversial: other news stories may split the audience into advocates and critics but no one is likely to be in favour of natural disasters or other damage to nature. Where audience and advertising revenues matter, such considerations are bound to influence reporting.

Because most environmental issues are closely connected to complex scientific arguments it is also extremely difficult for the public to evaluate them critically. The increasing distance that separates the production of knowledge by specialists and its reception by a broader lay public is an inevitable consequence of the advancement of human knowledge. While it was still possible for a well-educated person in the eighteenth century to have a good understanding of virtually all the scientific innovations of the time, this is no longer possible today. Obsolete scientific findings or misrepresentations of scientific findings can therefore survive and remain influential in public debates in a way that they cannot in the scientific arena.

Environmental issues are not only complex but they are also morally charged. Virtually everyone will agree that protecting the environment is a good thing. This is in part an achievement of the green movement. But this also has negative consequences for the openness of the debate. In the face of a strong social consensus about environmental protection, most people will not want to expose themselves to the accusation of taking green matters lightly. As a result, too many hard questions remain unasked, thus lowering the quality of the debate.

These and a number of other mechanisms lead to distorted reporting and public debates. But Lomborg also suggests that the problem does not only lie with the 'supply side'. He speculates that humans are particularly receptive to bad news about the environment. The success of green doomsayers fits into a longer cultural tradition that reflects mankind's fear of its own achievements: 'In a sense, when we have done so very well, maybe we ought to be punished? In that light, the worry over global warming could be seen as a search for nemesis, to punish our overconsumption, a penalty for our playing the Sorcerer's Apprentice.'[16]

Green thought therefore appears as a part of a long tradition of consumption critique, some parts of which have been discussed in previous chapters. Some green authors deliberately stress this continuity: the chapters of *The Limits to Growth* have short epigraphs that are – with only one exception – chosen from the writings of ancient Greek philosophers or the Bible. Among them, there is a lengthy quote in which Aristotle expounds his views about the need for moderation in consumption and lifestyle that we examined in the first chapter. And while it would be anachronistic to describe Aristotle as a green thinker, there can be little doubt that he would have approved of one of the central tenets of green thought, namely that the ideal state of humanity is an equilibrium state characterised by the absence of growth and excessive appetites.

Given the continuities among the proponents of abstinence, it is not surprising that some of the rhetoric used by critics of green thought today resembles that of earlier defenders of progress. In 1736 Voltaire invited his readers to forget about the Golden Age of the past when humanity allegedly lived in frugal simplicity. Instead, he called on his contemporaries to enjoy the pleasures and material comforts that present and future had to offer. Lomborg concludes his 1998 critique of green austerity on a similar note, with a spirited defence of humanity's present material achievements and future prospects:

Think about it. When would you prefer to have been born? ... This is the very message of [this] book: children born today – in both the industrialized world and developing countries – will live longer and be healthier, they will get more food, a better education, a higher standard of living, more leisure time and far more possibilities – without the global environment destroyed. And that is a beautiful world.[17]

CHAPTER 8

Is greed good?

For the past 2,500 years proponents of austerity have mostly failed to make a convincing economic case for their cause. Perhaps the only instance in which the tools of economic analysis have successfully been used to show a connection between abstinence and growth has been in the context of industrialisation. But even there abstinence from consumption as a precondition for capital accumulation was only half of the economic story: the other half was about expanding markets and a new consumer culture.

Does this mean that we can safely ignore the voices that have called for restraint in consumption because they have 'only' religious, moral and political arguments to offer? Certainly not. Economics, as it is conceived today, has a very narrow focus. When it is successful it can answer the question 'How do we maximise growth?' This is not a minor question, in particular in periods of economic crisis, and the lack of a compelling economic rationale for today's austerity policies should be a sufficient motive to end them sooner rather than later. However, we also need to consider the future of consumption beyond the current crisis and in the broader historical context of the extraordinarily high level of affluence which the industrialised countries have reached.

Economics is singularly unsuited to this purpose. In its current form it cannot engage in a meaningful way with the question 'Do we need more growth?' This is, however, a crucial question. In the words of Erich Fromm, we must not allow the question 'What is good for the growth of the system?' to overshadow the question 'What is good for Man?'[1] Economics can only tell us about means but not about ends. If we want to answer questions about the ultimate ends of economic activity we need to look beyond economics.

This chapter reviews some of the most powerful non-economic arguments in favour of abstinence and asks how our consumption habits would have to change if we were to take them seriously and adopt a form of 'ethical austerity', based on the teachings of Western philosophy. We will also ask how such an 'ethical austerity' would compare with the austerity policies of today. However, before addressing this question we will briefly discuss how economics as a discipline lost the ability to engage with normative questions.

The science of economics

Economic thought has not always been as limited in its scope. For much of human history, perspectives on economic matters were dominated by normative arguments, while considerations of economic efficiency were entirely absent. The perspectives of Aristotle and the Christian tradition are good examples of this. Economic debates began to move away from normative questions when economics established itself as a discipline distinct from other branches of philosophical or social enquiry towards the end of the eighteenth century.

However, even after the first chairs of political economy had been established and a more important body of specifically economic theory had been gradually created, significant traces of moral, historical and political thought continued to be present in economic discussions. The nineteenth-century exchanges about primitive accumulation illustrate this: Smith, Weber, Marx and Veblen not only differed in their understanding of the mechanics of the economic process; they also disagreed fundamentally in their interpretations of the historical context and in the moral judgements they passed. The contentious questions were who the heroes and villains of industrialisation were and how we should judge the social and economic system which the process of industrialisation produced.

However, similar issues were almost completely ignored once economics began to reinvent itself as a science. Towards the end of the nineteenth century the rise of the neoclassical school of economics meant that economists now focused on understanding how markets worked. To this end the institutional and historical contexts were excluded as far as possible from the analysis. Henceforth, economics studied an idealised, perfected version of the market process. This heroic act allowed a leap in the understanding of markets. But at the same time, economics began to lose touch with reality to some extent. The discipline began to ignore many of the institutional, political and historical questions that are fundamental to the practice of economic actors. Moreover, and most importantly for our purposes, it was at this stage of development that economics almost completely ceased to engage with moral issues.

By becoming more like a natural science, economics began fully to share the predicament of the scientific culture created by the Enlightenment. Max Horkheimer and Theodor Adorno have discussed this problem under the heading of the 'dialectic of Enlightenment': from the seventeenth century, Enlightenment thinkers radically scrutinised the existing beliefs and explanatory models. Only what could be supported by empirically verifiable, preferably measurable facts was accepted. The rest was discarded. This process made it possible to build a much more accurate understanding of the world. Initially, the natural world was at the centre of these efforts but much progress was also made in understanding societies and political systems by using empirical methods.

Sometimes Enlightenment thinkers took their project too far to be useful: Montesquieu's experiments with sheep's tongues, discussed in *The Spirit of the Laws*, did not add much to his argument. Nonetheless, the rest of Montesquieu's enquiry, into the effects of climatic and geographic factors, led to a much more complete understanding of social and political structures and their evolution. The empirical method also demonstrated its power in the social sciences.

Armed with the power of empiricism the Enlightenment demolished much of the mythological worldview and thus liberated man from his 'self imposed tutelage'. But the concentration on empiricism also left the Enlightenment open to the charge of neglecting everything that was not amenable to empirical proof, such as moral and ethical standards. As an example of this problem we can think of the moral imperative: 'thou shall not kill.' It is generally accepted, but impossible to prove empirically. On the contrary, it is easy to imagine scenarios where it would be perfectly rational to ignore this commandment: consider how many individuals in need of organ transplants could be saved by killing a single person and using their organs, or how the killing of elderly people would solve many problems of today's pension systems and alleviate financial pressure on younger generations. In such cases, cool rationality combined with the aim to maximise happiness could be used to justify murder. Still, most people would reject such a course of action on moral grounds.

When Voltaire exclaimed 'if God did not exist, one would have to invent him' he was not being cynical.[2] He was pointing to an important shortcoming of the Enlightenment tradition, namely its difficulty in providing sound foundations for ethical standards. Despite being frequently accused of atheism, Voltaire and many other exponents of the Enlightenment tradition believed that morality could ultimately rest only on religious foundations.

By becoming more 'scientific', economics has made great progress in understanding the 'mechanics' of the market process, but this focus has also led it to be ill-equipped to provide answers about the ends of economic activity. Modern economics centres on the procedural question of how limitless wants can best be satisfied with limited resources. Whether wants should be limitless or, if not, what the limits should be, it cannot answer. Equally, economics has no answer to the question of whether all wants should be satisfied and in what order.

Economics as a moral science

Some modern economists have tried to venture beyond the limits of their discipline as it is defined today in order to answer normative questions. We have discussed Keynes's tract about the 'Economic possibilities for our grandchildren', and the way in which Hayek built his entire argument on one supreme ethical imperative, the preservation of liberty. In the late 1950s, John Kenneth Galbraith explored the limits of consumption in *The Affluent Society*; in the 1970s Ernst Friedrich Schumacher published his influential *Small Is Beautiful: A Study of Economics as if People Mattered*; and recently the historian Robert Skidelsky and the philosopher Edward Skidelsky jointly explored similar questions in their book *How Much Is Enough?*

Many modern economic thinkers who engage with ethical questions turn back to the ideas of pre-modern philosophers and to religious traditions. Keynes expected a return to 'principles of religion and traditional virtue' once the economic problem had been solved.[3] The Skidelskys, like Keynes, propose a version of Aristotle's 'good life' in their discussion of the ultimate ends of economic activity. They also suggest that a revival of Christian social thought may be necessary in order to bring about an ethical transformation on a broad scale.

Often, the point of departure for ethical considerations is Aristotle's insight that the accumulation of money or wealth cannot be an end in itself. This is because money is only useful in so far as it can be exchanged for something else. At the same time, everything that is intrinsically useful cannot be sensibly accumulated without limits. The need that makes it useful will at some point be satisfied, making any further acquisition of the good futile. This powerful argument forces us to consider not only the means to economic growth but also its ends.

However, if we accept that there ought to be limits to growth on ethical grounds, this also affects the terms in which we need to think about consumption: many of the arguments against abstinence hinge on the importance of expanding consumption for continued growth. Moreover, if we accept that human needs are finite, this must lead to thinking about the limits of consumption. Once maximising growth is no longer the supreme economic goal, we need to define other criteria in order to decide 'how much is enough' with regard to consumption. We also need to think about what forms of consumption society should aspire to.

This is an important question but it is also one that applies today to only a small part of the world. Most of humanity is still faced with scarcity of food and basic consumption goods and will, reasonably, care mainly about the maximisation of growth. However, in the West, which is what this book is about, it may be argued that we have now reached a level of material wealth that has effectively solved the economic problem. If we look at statistical averages rather than at actual distribution, there clearly is enough wealth to ensure a comfortable life for everyone in most countries in the West.

This is true despite the economic crisis that is currently affecting the industrialised nations. With the right policies – most importantly, perhaps, an end to austerity – substantial growth could be brought back relatively quickly. But even if policies that stymie growth remain in place, there will be a modest recovery at some point as a result of cyclical fluctuations: the upswing will come later and will be weaker than would be possible with better policies, and growth may well remain sluggish for years or even decades. Secular economic stagnation may be enough to lead to disastrous political consequences and to ruin the lives of many. Nonetheless, the overall level of prosperity is high and will continue to rise in the

Western world and this means that we have to face the question of 'how much is enough'. When Keynes contemplated this question he was thinking of the economic prospects of his grandchildren. Today, time horizons are different. We can no longer pass the buck to future generations. The time has come to decide these matters.

If we accept that unlimited growth can no longer be our goal, what kind of economic ends should society pursue? And if limits to consumption are desirable on moral grounds, what would a programme of austerity guided by ethical principles look like in practice? Some of the arguments for abstinence that we have discussed here provide useful cues. In particular, the perspectives of Aristotle, of Hayek and of the environmental thinkers are valuable sources of inspiration. However, they were in part formulated in times that were very different from ours. We therefore have to 'translate' their advice for contemporary use and ask how patterns of consumption would need to change today if we were to take seriously the ethical teachings from the past. The list is hardly exhaustive but should be seen as a contribution to a wider debate about the ends of economic activity.[4]

Leisure and friendship

Aristotle proposes that leading the 'good life' is man's ultimate purpose on earth and suggests that two of the most important ingredients of this way of life are friendship and leisure. The high importance that he accords to friendship is easy to understand. Leisure is a less intuitive concept. At one level it means time off work. This is an important aspect: excessively long working hours will leave little time and energy to pursue a fulfilling and happy life. But in Aristotle's understanding leisure is more than free time. It is not mere idleness. Leisure is characterised by activity and the pursuit of an objective that is autonomously chosen. Crucially, the satisfaction derived from leisure must be intrinsic to the activity. Work that gives satisfaction because of the money earned or the prestige gained does not qualify as leisure. But most hobbies do. Only if the activity gives pleasure of itself, independent of external motivations, can we speak of leisure. This self-sufficiency is a crucial quality that makes leisure an indispensable ingredient of the good life. Life without leisure is 'a life spent always in the preparation, never in actual living'.[5] Certain forms of paid work can be considered leisure if the external rewards received, economic and otherwise, are not the primary motive for pursuing them. However, in practice not many jobs fit that description. Therefore a limitation of labour time is a precondition to ensuring that leisure is given due space in life.

Another consequence is that work needs to become more similar to leisure where possible. The principal distinction between the two is the autonomous control that is typical of leisure activities and the external control that is usually associated with work. Those who work in contexts where they control much of the work process autonomously or where they have at least a significant say in important decisions are a fortunate minority. Their experience at work gives them more satisfaction and causes less stress. They are less exposed to certain aspects of what Marx termed 'alienation'. In order to give prominence to the values of leisure it is not only necessary to curtail the time spent at work; it is also necessary to give those who work more of a say in how work environments and work processes are organised. A fully 'democratic economy' may be utopian but greater participation and representation of workers will go a long way to making sure that workplaces are tailored to human needs and not only to economic imperatives.

Complex issues arise from the fact that leisure time is not merely time off work. As Keynes warned, additional free time may lead individuals to reflect on the meaninglessness of their existence and face a nervous breakdown – he used the example of the 'wives of the well-to-do classes'.[6] However, the problem may be not so much one of gender and class as one of growing up without sufficiently experiencing the pleasures of leisure. Today, many children are put through an intense educational programme from an early age. In particular, the unfortunate offspring of middle-class overachievers across the Western world are put through demanding schools and after-school activities. Quite apart from the problem that from early on in their lives children are left with little time that they can auton- omously fill, much of the education that they receive is contrary to the ideals of leisure. Much of the efforts of parents and educational institutions are geared towards ensuring that the children's economic success later in life is on a par with, or, ideally, superior to that of their parents. Therefore, there is too much focus on teaching marketable skills. Education of this type is a mere preparation for future economic success. Often enough it fails even at this narrow goal. Worse still, it neglects the full development of individual personalities and interests and does not allow children to experience the pleasure of activities undertaken for their own sake.

How, then, can new generations be equipped to enjoy leisure? Children are normally playful, curious and derive great satisfaction from pursuits that serve no ulterior purpose.

Humans seem therefore naturally suited to leisure. Spending less time to rid them of these innate qualities in schools and universities may go a long way to preparing humankind for a more leisurely future. In this sense, an important role can be played by an adequately funded educational system that has the capacity to cater to the talents of individuals. The ethos of such a system needs to be about educating the mind and developing personalities rather than training for specific purposes. Many of the best schools work on similar premises. However, economic barriers often limit access. This needs to be changed and access to education and individual educational trajectories need to be determined as a function of the talents and needs of individuals. In addition to reforming education, leisure can be promoted by building on long traditions of communal activities that exist everywhere in the Western world. Sports clubs, music groups and many types of associations that pursue activities for the fun of doing so need only be given adequate support to thrive further.

Friendship is much more difficult to promote than leisure because of its intimate nature. However, the two goods are closely related and communal leisure activities provide an environment where friendships can develop. With regard to economic life the value of friendship exists to some extent in tension with the requirements of modern economies. The high degree of flexibility that is expected of many workers today often gets in the way of the creation of stable and satisfying interpersonal relationships. Individuals who are forced by the labour market to move repeatedly during their lifetimes are less likely to be able to maintain a circle of close friends with whom they can share the events of their lives. For some, mobility is a choice and it can then be a rewarding experience, but often it is not. In order to promote the value of friendship, less, not more, mobility is necessary.

Already today, friendship and leisure are important parts of the lives of most people in the West and elsewhere. However, how would it affect our patterns of consumption if we were to really take them seriously as guiding principles of our economic life? The basic precondition for leisure is a limitation of working hours. As a result of trade union pressure and governmental regulation, working times have substantially decreased since the early days of industrialisation. In the early nineteenth century, average working hours in Germany and many other industrialising nations were in excess of 80 hours per week. By the turn of the century this had dropped to 60 hours and today average weekly working hours are below 40 in most industrialised countries.

This development reflects the fact that over the decades a part of the growing productivity of human labour resulting from technological progress has not been used to increase output but to shorten working hours. Keynes expected this process to continue so that by 2030 the average working time would have reached fifteen hours per week. However, actual outcomes have been different. Working hours have declined more slowly than Keynes expected, despite sustained productivity growth. In other words, more of the growing productivity has been used to produce more goods and less to shorten working hours.

However, the additional production did not always lead to a rapid growth in wages either. In particular, since the political shift of the early 1980s, a growing share of productivity growth has contributed to increasing the profits of companies and shareholders and the salaries of a small group of privileged workers at the top. The much discussed gap between the growth of the incomes of the top 1 per cent of income earners and the rest is one manifestation of this development. In order to prioritise leisure, this trend would have to be changed. More of productivity growth needs to be used to shorten working hours while keeping salaries stable. As a consequence, high incomes and profits would be reduced, or increase at low rates.

What would this mean for patterns of consumption? Since real wages of most workers would remain unchanged they would not have to change their habits of consumption. But they would have more leisure time. And if additional services are provided as part of the efforts to promote leisure activities, most individuals would actually consume more. (The aim of such services would have to be to promote active and self-guided activity rather than passively consumed entertainment. Still, in an economic sense, even the theatre mentor who helps a group of amateurs to stage a play is an item on the consumption inventory of the participants.)

In contrast, high-income earners would most likely have to change their consumption habits as a result of a decline in their incomes. Higher incomes are usually not entirely spent on consumption. A decline in income would therefore mean a decline in saving and consumption. Some top earners who would have to change their consumption habits as a result of 'ethical austerity' might perceive this as an undue sacrifice. However, many would also appreciate the new situation that afforded a break from competing with their peers for the latest item of conspicuous consumption. 'Ethical austerity' would also remove much of the incentive to spend extra hours or weekends in the office, and thus bring the benefits of leisure not only to the toiling masses but also to high-flying executives and their families

In an age of globalisation a similar paradigm shift would raise many economic questions that go beyond the national context. Would more leisure for workers not mean companies that are less competitive and hence less able to survive against international competition from places where lowering costs remains the priority? Will top executives who are paid less not take their skills elsewhere? The degree of global mobility of goods, services and individuals is perhaps sometimes exaggerated, but some of these pressures would certainly be felt. A degree of 'de-globalisation' may be a precondition for a reconstruction of economies according to ethical principles.[7]

Liberty

From Hayek and his precursor Wilhelm von Humboldt we take the message that liberty is a crucial element of the 'good life'. This is a compelling argument. Freedom from oppression, the opportunity to live through a variety of experiences, the ability to live by one's own plan and to enjoy the respect of fellow members of one's community are preconditions to living a fulfilling live.

Individual liberty has lost none of its importance since the times of Humboldt and Hayek. However, the nexus between the rise of strong states and a loss of individual liberty they both constructed seems with hindsight to be simplistic. Humboldt wrote in part against the overbearing paternalism of Prussian absolutism in the late eighteenth century. He was also concerned at the power of a revolutionary government in France that, carried on a wave of popular support, felt little need to curtail the range of its activities. Hayek in turn wrote after he had witnessed the oppression and devastation caused in Europe by fascist states in the 1930s and 1940s. It is easy to see how their historical contexts inspired a profound mistrust of the institution of the state. There can be no doubt that in history states have in many instances been the enemies of individual liberty.

However, states have also been champions of liberty in other periods. During the post-war decades many Western states have successfully protected and extended the liberties of their citizens. Institutions of modern states have in this period enabled their citizens to live freer and fuller lives than would have been possible without these states. Often states also played ambiguous roles: on 4 September 1957, the Arkansas National Guard prevented a group of black students from attending Little Rock Central High School. But on 24 September, another organ of the American state, the 101st Airborne Division enabled the students to attend the school. Any reflection on the question of whether the state has been an agent of oppression or liberation in this instance is further complicated by the fact that the school would most likely not have existed without the contribution of a developed and sizeable system of government.

In the light of a complex historical experience, it is simplistic to single out the state as an enemy of liberty. In practice, much depends on the nature of the state and the goals which it pursues. Consequently, the notion that a small state is always better suited to the protection of individual liberty does not sufficiently capture the complexity of the interaction between state and individual. Rather than prescribing blanket abstinence to the state it is necessary to look in more detail at how different types of state expenditure limit and enhance individual liberty.

A more nuanced understanding of the relation between state action and individual liberty can be reached by considering Roosevelt's notion of the Four Freedoms. The president developed this perspective on liberty in 1941, at the same time as Hayek was working on *The Road to Serfdom*. Both discussions of liberty were intended to outline the goals of democratic societies and contrast them with the sinister ends of the fascist and Stalinist dictatorships of the time. However, while Hayek's concept of liberty was compatible with the first two of Roosevelt's freedoms (freedom of speech and worship), the latter two (freedom from want and fear) went well beyond traditional liberal values.

A priori, freedom of speech and freedom of religion seem to be unrelated to the economic ends of society. However, this is only true if they are understood in a narrow way. If we accept that freedom of speech also includes a right to be heard, then a whole range of implications develops. Seen in this way, freedom of speech also guarantees that individuals will have a say in the important decisions that affect their lives. Democratic political participation is inseparable from freedom of speech.

However, questions of political power are intimately linked to economic power. In electoral campaigns and legislative processes, the voice of money can often be heard along with that of the electorate. In such instances, as in many others, the egalitarian principles of democracy exist in tension with economic inequality. This always poses a challenge but it does not necessarily lead to fundamental problems. Only if economic inequality becomes extreme is it likely to become a burden for the stability of a political system built on equality. In part, this is because the interests of citizens with very different amounts of wealth and income diverge widely and this makes it more difficult to find consensus.

More importantly, growing economic inequality also means that the role of the state as the guardian and protector of private property becomes an increasingly uncomfortable one. As Rousseau pointed out, excessive economic inequality is bound to turn any political order into an oppressive one. Where high economic inequality exists, the primary objective of the state is to protect the wealthy from the envy and rage of the majority. One alternative to such a repressive scenario is to convince the majority that even a high degree of inequality is legitimate.[8] Another way to resolve the tension between democracy and inequality is to use political means to reach a more equal distribution of wealth.

Freedom from want and fear are in more obvious ways related to economic ends and means. These freedoms are, however, not merely a guarantee for health and full physical development. They also play a fundamental role in allowing individuals to live through a wide variety of experiences with an open mind. Nothing closes the mind more than fear of crime and a constant concern about how to make ends meet. Only when individuals have solved their economic problems can they devote time, attention and interest to more uplifting pursuits.

Moreover, individuals must also be free from the fear that this stable situation may suddenly end. At its most banal, they need to be free of the fear that their life or their property may be taken from them by a criminal. However, given that most people do not live off their property, job loss is a much more common type of existential threat than theft. Freedom from fear therefore also has a significant economic dimension, which includes secure employment and an adequate safety net for those who lose their jobs.

Today Western societies have reached a level of prosperity that allows them to guarantee all citizens freedom from want and fear. However, while this is true in the world of statistical averages, it is in contrast with the actual experience of many inhabitants of the Western world. There are still substantial numbers of people whose access to the material comforts is far below average and who lack access to basic goods and services. It is true that only very small numbers live in misery. Most of those who are considered to be poor by the standards of industrialised countries would be considered fortunate in other parts of the world. However, poverty is inevitably a relative concept; there is little point in dwelling on the fact that the even poorest English people today would have been considered wonders of prosperity at the time of the Norman Conquest. If we accept freedom from fear and want as economic ends, then acceptable levels of consumption and security have to be defined in the context of the capabilities and aspirations of today's advanced societies.

The main economic consequence of accepting the four freedoms as goals of society would be a more equal distribution of incomes. How would this affect patterns of consumption? On the one hand, one should expect a substantial increase at the lower end of the income scale, mainly among welfare recipients but also for recipients of lower wages. This increase would correspond to a decrease or slow growth in higher incomes and profits. The decline in higher incomes would partly lead to a reduction in consumption by these groups. Additional consumption by the poorer would therefore, once again, correspond to greater austerity among the wealthier, leaving overall consumption unchanged. However, a decline in higher incomes would also lead to a decline in the amount saved by these groups. Instead of being saved by the better off, these funds would now be spent by the less prosperous. Greater equality would therefore most likely lead to an overall increase in consumption. Incidentally, such a shift in income distribution would also go a long way to solving some of the problems associated with the 'paradox of thrift' that plague advanced economies.

Green values

Green thought, too, can contribute important elements to a debate about the objectives which societies should pursue. The aim of protecting the environment has today become one of the most widely accepted goals in Western societies. Different individuals have come to accept this conclusion for different reasons, but there is comparatively little controversy about the view that nature deserves protection and respect. There is, however, substantial disagreement about the means to achieve this end. Many green thinkers believe that punitive and far-reaching abstinence from consumption is necessary. However, close examination of the evidence does not always bear out such views. As more optimistic commentators point out, inventiveness may well be able to solve this challenge just as it has helped humanity to overcome many other problems in the past.

If technology is to provide the solutions to at least some of our environmental problems then large-scale investments are required, for example in a shift to renewable energy. Such a change can most likely not be brought about without state intervention. Market structures are not adapted to it because the pricing mechanism is unable to capture important parts of the relevant information. Moreover, the risks and volumes of the necessary investment are often too great for private investors and profits may not always match those of other, non-green, investment opportunities. However, if states act directly, a sufficiently rapid and far-reaching shift seems possible. This would hardly be a new phenomenon: historically, states have often played important roles in processes of fundamental technological change.

If Western societies decide to devote substantial resources to ecological ends, the outcome might well be that in the future our showers will be as hot and our beers as cold as they are now, only the energy will come from different, less harmful sources. In such an optimistic vision we may still be able to go from A to B and perhaps even faster than today; only we might use a self-driving electric car that is part of a car-sharing pool, or a high-speed train instead of the conventional car or plane that we would use today. All of this would require a degree of change in individual habits of consumption. But mainly it would require substantial political change that leads to large-scale investment and structural economic change.

The scale of investment required for such structural economic shifts could, in theory, drain resources from consumption. Abstinence from consumption was necessary during the period of industrialisation in Europe in order to free sufficient resources for the accumulation of productive capital. However, this time may be different. Today economies are much larger than in the nineteenth century and can devote much larger sums to investment without having to impose abstinence on consumers. On the contrary, the fundamental problem of developed economies is that investment opportunities are lacking for the increasing amounts that are being saved. Green investments may be a good outlet for these savings. In this way savings and investments could be brought into balance without having to resort to lowering savings through the painful mechanism of declining incomes.

Not least, we should also consider the ecological implications of prioritising leisure over additional material consumption. Additional resources yielded by productivity growth would in part be used for green investments. But the part of productivity growth earmarked for consumption would be used to reduce labour time instead of increasing material consumption. Substantial benefits for the environment could therefore be expected from a more leisurely lifestyle.

Conclusion

This list of ethical objectives is hardly comprehensive. Also, no matter how much respect we may have for the wisdom of the great thinkers of the past, the details, practical implications and the legitimacy of the economic goals of society can ultimately only be decided by democratic processes in the present. Such processes are slow and prone to make mistakes. Indeed, as the Skidelskys point out, many of the democratically elected governments of the last decades have moved us further away from attaining the 'elements of the good life' instead of bringing societies closer to them.

However, there is also reason for hope. One principal means to move society closer to the ideals of the 'good life' is greater economic equality. The historical evidence shows that, at least in the long run, more democratic participation is normally associated with greater redistribution from rich to poor. Historically, the more democratic states of North America have developed more redistributive fiscal systems than the countries of South America. Similarly, historical evidence shows that increases in the democratic franchise in Europe during the nineteenth and twentieth centuries have in most cases led to more redistributive fiscal patterns. Like most improvements in the human condition, the 'good life' is unlikely to happen by itself. Deeply entrenched social and economic structures as well as powerful vested interests are obstacles to the necessary change. However, those who wish to bring humanity closer to the 'good life' may find that democracy provides them with a powerful lever.

While it is not immediately clear what exactly the 'good life' would look like and how it can be brought about, it is evident that forms of abstinence from consumption will play an important role in this new way of life. However, such an 'ethical austerity' would look very different from the policies that are implemented today under the heading of 'austerity'. National experiences differ, but today the brunt of expenditure cuts falls on pensions, welfare payments, the salaries of government employees and other government services. The result is that the current version of austerity is affecting mostly those with average and below average incomes. In contrast, 'ethical austerity' as discussed here would negatively affect mainly those with higher incomes and profits. For large parts of society, a revision of consumption patterns based on ethical imperatives would not be an exercise in austerity at all, and for many it would even mean an increase in levels of consumption.

The conclusions of this survey of the last 2,500 years of debate about abstinence are sobering: there are no convincing economic arguments for austerity policies in their current form and there is no compelling moral or political case for them either. Austerity, in its current form, is simply a great failure.

Notes

Chapter 1 Austere ideas for austere societies: from Aristotle to Aquinas

1. Diogenes Laertius, *The Lives of the Eminent Philosophers* (2 vols, Cambridge, MA, 1925), vol. 1, p. 445.
2. Aristotle, *The Politics* (London, 1992), I: iv, p. 64.
3. In *To Have or To Be*, Erich Fromm points to the philosopher Aristippus as a possible exception. However, we only know about the views of this disciple of Socrates indirectly via the writings of Laertius and others.
4. Aristotle, *The Nicomachean Ethics* (Oxford, 2009), III: 10, p. 56.
5. Aristotle, *Ethics*, III: 10, pp. 55–6.
6. Aristotle, *Ethics*, III: 11, p. 57.
7. Aristotle, *Ethics*, III: 12, p. 59.
8. Aristotle, *Ethics*, IV: 1, p. 60.
9. Aristotle, *Ethics*, IV: 2, p. 66.
10. Aristotle, *Ethics*, IV: 2, p. 66.
11. Aristotle, *Politics*, I: x, p. 86.
12. Immanuel Kant, *Grounding for the Metaphysics of Morals* (Indianapolis, IN, 1993), p. 30.
13. Matthew 6: 24.
14. Matthew 6: 19.
15. Matthew 6: 31.
16. Matthew 6: 32.
17. Stephen Long, *Christian Ethics. A Very Short Introduction* (Oxford, 2010), p. 109.
18. Ezekiel 16: 49–50.
19. Mark 10: 25.
20. John Maynard Keynes, *The General Theory of Employment, Interest and Money*, vol. 7 of *The Collected Writings of John Maynard Keynes* (Cambridge, 2013), p. 383.

Chapter 2 Austerity v. reason: from Mandeville to Voltaire

1. Adam Smith, *An Inquiry into the Wealth of Nations*, ed. Roy Campbell and Andrew Skinner (2 vols, Indianapolis, IN, 1981), vol. 1, p. 342.

2. Cited in Robert Heilbroner, *Teachings from the Worldly Philosophy* (New York, 1996), p. 19.
3. Bernard Mandeville, *The Fable of the Bees or Private Vices, Publick Benefits* (2 vols, Indianapolis, IN, 1988), vol. 1, p. 128.
4. Mandeville, *Fable*, vol. 1, p. 129.
5. Voltaire, 'The man of the world', in John Morley, *The Works of Voltaire: A Contemporary Version*, trans. William F. Fleming, annotated Tobias Smollett (21 vols, New York, 1901), vol. 10.
6. Mandeville, *Fable*, vol. 1, p. 67.
7. Mandeville, *Fable*, vol. 1, p. 69.
8. Mandeville, *Fable*, vol. 1, p. 73.
9. Voltaire, 'The worldling', in Morley, *The Works of Voltaire*, vol. 10.
10. Mandeville, *Fable*, vol. 1, p. 69.
11. Mandeville, *Fable*, vol. 1, p. 108.

Chapter 3　Austerity for capitalism: from Smith to Weber

1. Smith, *Wealth of Nations*, vol. 1, p. 254.
2. Smith, *Wealth of Nations*, vol. 1, p. 324.
3. Smith, *Wealth of Nations*, vol. 1, p. 108.
4. Weber's argument is complicated by the great number of different 'brands' of Protestantism. We shall focus here on his comments on Calvinism, which encapsulate the essence of his views.
5. Karl Marx, *Capital* (3 vols, Marx/Engels Internet Archive, 2010), vol. 1, p. 532.
6. Marx, *Capital*, vol. 1, p. 500.
7. Marx, *Capital*, vol. 1, p. 118.

Chapter 4　Austerity for stability: from the Great War to the next

1. Stanley Baldwin cited in Barry Eichengreen and Peter Temin, 'Fetters of gold and paper', *Oxford Review of Economic Policy*, 3 (2010), p. 376.
2. Winston Churchill cited in Liaquat Ahamed, *Lords of Finance: The Bankers Who Broke the World* (London, 2009), p. 232.
3. Barry Eichengreen and Peter Temin, 'The gold standard and the Great Depression', *Contemporary European History*, 2 (2000), p. 183.
4. Ahamed, *Lords of Finance*, p. 155.
5. Ahamed, *Lords of Finance*, p. 169.
6. Stanley Baldwin cited in Ahamed, *Lords of Finance*, p. 431.
7. Barry Eichengreen and Peter Temin have discussed the parallels between the limitations imposed by the gold standard and the euro in their thoughtful article: 'Fetters of gold and paper'.
8. Joseph Schumpeter, 'Die Grenzen der Lohnpolitik', *Der Deutsche Volkswirt*, 3 (1928), p. 848. Translated by the author.
9. Initially, Brüning's political options were also limited by the reparations regime imposed by the victors of the First World War but in 1931 the Hoover moratorium led to the suspension of international debt and reparations payments. To what extent viable alternatives to Brüning's economic policies existed in the light of international financial obliga-

tions remains controversial among economic historians. (see the contributions of Harold James, Knut Borchardt and Albrecht Ritschl among others).

10. Article in the journal *Der Arbeitgeber* (The employer) cited in Bernd Weisbrod, *Schwerindustrie in der Weimarer Republik* (Wuppertal, 1978), p. 396. Translated by the author.

11. J. Herle, 'Das Problem der Wirtschaftsdemokratie auf der Düsseldorfer Industrietagung 1929', in *Das Problem der Wirtschaftsdemokratie. Zur Düsseldorfer Tagung des Reichsverbandes der deutschen Industrie* (Düsseldorf, 1929), pp. 5–8. Translated by the author.

12. Herle, 'Das Problem der Wirtschaftsdemokratie', p. 5. Translated by the author.

13. New York banker R. C. Leffingwell cited in Harold James, *The German Slump: Politics and Economics 1924–36* (Oxford, 1986), p. 16.

Chapter 5 Austerity can wait: Keynes

1. Thomas Robert Malthus, *Principles of Political Economy*, cited in Keynes, *General Theory*, p. 363.

2. Keynes, *General Theory*, p. 364.

3. John Mackinnon Robertson cited in Robert Nash and William Gramm, 'A neglected early statement of the paradox of thrift', *History of Political Economy*, 1 (1969), p. 397.

4. This and the following citations are from Friedrich Hayek, 'The "paradox" of saving', *Economica*, 32 (1931), p. 125.

5. Franklin Delano Roosevelt, 'One third of a nation', Second Inaugural Address, 20 Jan. 1937; Joseph Dorfman, *The Economic Mind in American Civilization*, vol. 4 (New York, 1959), p. 345.

6. Joan Robinson, 'The second crisis of economic theory', *American Economic Review*, 62 (1972), p. 8.

7. Keynes, *General Theory*, p. 84.

8. Keynes, *General Theory*, p. 167 (emphasis added).

9. Keynes, *General Theory*, p. 174 (emphasis added).

10. Keynes, *General Theory*, p. 111.

11. Keynes, *General Theory*, p. 129.

12. John Maynard Keynes, 'How to avoid a slump', in Donald Moggridge, ed., *The Collected Writings of John Maynard Keynes*, vol. 21: *Activities 1931–1939: World Crises and Policies in Britain and America* (London, 1982), p. 390. Originally published in *The Times*, 12–14 Jan. 1937.

13. Keynes, *General Theory*, p. 164.

14. Keynes, John Maynard, 'Economic possibilities for our grandchildren', in Donald Moggridge, ed., *The Collected Writings of John Maynard Keynes*, vol. 9: *Essays in Persuasion* (London, 1972), p. 322.

15. Keynes cited in Robert Skidelsky, *The Return of the Master* (London, 2010), p. 153.

16. Skidelsky, *Return of the Master*, pp. 146, 157.

17. John Maynard Keynes, 'The general theory of employment', *Quarterly Journal of Economics*, 51 (1937), p. 213.

18. Keynes, 'General theory of employment', p. 214.

19. Keynes, 'General theory of employment', p. 215.
20. Friedrich Hayek, 'The road from serfdom', interview with Thomas W. Hazlett, 1977, *Reason Magazine* (July 1992).
21. George Edward Moore cited in Victoria Chick, 'Economics and the good life: Keynes and Schumacher', paper, World Economics Association conference, 2012, p. 6.
22. Aristotle, *The Politics*, p. 64.
23. Keynes cited in Chick, 'Economics and the good life', p. 2.
24. Keynes, 'Economic possibilities', p. 328.
25. Keynes, 'Economic possibilities', p. 331.
26. Keynes, 'Economic possibilities', p. 331.

Chapter 6 Austerity for the state: Hayek

1. Margaret Thatcher cited in Nicholas Wapshott, *Keynes Hayek: The Clash that Defined Modern Economics* (London, 2011), p. 258.
2. Friedrich Hayek cited in Alan Ebenstein, *Friedrich Hayek: A Biography* (New York, 2001), p. 291.
3. Wapshott, *Keynes Hayek*, p. 140
4. Friedrich Hayek et al., 'Public works from rates', Letter to the editor, *The Times* (of London), 19 Oct. 1932, p. 10.
5. Milton Friedman, 'Mr Market' (interview), *Hoover Digest*, 1 (1999).
6. Wapshott, *Keynes Hayek*, p. 172.
7. John Maynard Keynes, *A Tract on Monetary Reform* (Amherst, 2000), p. 80.
8. Friedrich Hayek, 'The road from serfdom', interview with Thomas W. Hazlett, 1977, *Reason Magazine* (July 1992).
9. Martin Wolf, 'Thatcher: the great transformer', *Financial Times*, 8 April 2013.
10. Friedrich Hayek, *The Road to Serfdom*, ed. Bruce Caldwell (Chicago, 2007), p. 127.
11. Hayek, *The Road to Serfdom*, pp. 97, 110.
12. Hayek, *The Road to Serfdom*, p. 37.
13. Frank Knight, 'Reader's report', in Hayek, *The Road to Serfdom*, p. 249.
14. Milton Friedman, cited in Wapshott, *Keynes Hayek*, p. 183.
15. Margaret Thatcher cited in Wapshott, *Keynes Hayek*, p. 259.

Chapter 7 Austerity for the planet: green ideas of consumption

1. Mary Shelley, *Frankenstein, or The Modern Prometheus* (Oxford, 2008).
2. George Monbiot, *Heat: How We Can Stop the Planet Burning* (London, 2007), p. 215.
3. Andrew Dobson, *Green Political Thought* (London, 2007), p. 25.
4. Donella Meadows et al., *The Limits to Growth: A Report for the Club of Rome's Project on the Predicament of Mankind* (London, 1974), p. 23.
5. Meadows et al., *Limits to Growth*, p. 29.
6. Meadows et al., *Limits to Growth*, p. 156.
7. Meadows et al., *Limits to Growth*, p. 175.
8. Meadows et al., *Limits to Growth*, p. 141.
9. Dobson, *Green Political Thought*, p. 122.
10. Marilyn Ferguson cited in Dobson, *Green Political Thought*, p. 122.

11. Dobson, *Green Political Thought*, p. 122.
12. Paul Ehrlich and Anne Ehrlich cited in Bjørn Lomborg, *The Skeptical Environmentalist: Measuring the Real State of the World* (Cambridge, 2012), p. 30.
13. Lomborg, *Skeptical Environmentalist*, p. 27.
14. Lomborg, *Skeptical Environmentalist*, p. 351.
15. Lomborg, *Skeptical Environmentalist*, p. 3.
16. Lomborg, *Skeptical Environmentalist*, p. 42.
17. Lomborg, *Skeptical Environmentalist*, p. 352.

Chapter 8 Is greed good?

1. Erich Fromm, *To Have or To Be* (New York, 1976), p. 6.
2. Voltaire cited in Peter Gay, *Voltaire's Politics: The Poet as a Realist* (New York, 1966), p. 265.
3. Keynes, 'Economic possibilities for our grandchildren', p. 331.
4. Despite some important differences, parts of the following owe a great debt to the excellent chapter 'Elements of the good life' in Robert and Edward Skidelsky's book *How Much Is Enough?* (London, 2012).
5. Skidelsky and Skidelsky, *How Much Is Enough?* p. 166.
6. Keynes, 'Economic possibilities', p. 327.
7. There is a short but insightful discussion of these issues at the end of Skidelsky and Skidelsky, *How Much Is Enough?*, pp. 211–18.
8. There is a long tradition of arguments to that effect in the history of economic thought: Smith and Weber justified inequality as the consequence of earlier abstinence, and Hayek defended inequality as a price for liberty. A further argument that has not been discussed here is the view of Francis Ysidoro Edgeworth, one of the leading economists of the late nineteenth century: for him inequality was justified because not all humans were equally able to appreciate the finer things in life. Greater wealth would therefore be wasted on the masses in general and on women in particular.

Bibliography

The bibliography is divided by chapters. Some entries are listed more than once because they are relevant to more than one chapter. Suggestions for general reading are listed in the first section.

Online sources are indicated where they are accessible for free. Libraries and universities often offer online access also to some of the other material, in particular to journal articles. The online versions indicated are not always identical with the print edition listed here; complete web addresses are indicated where the publication is only available in electronic form. For all other online resources only the website is indicated. A search on the website or a web search will bring up the relevant document. All urls given were valid as of September 2013.

Introduction

Baker, Dean, 'The myth of expansionary fiscal austerity', CEPR working paper (Oct. 2010). Online: http://www.cepr.net/documents/publications/austerity-myth-2010-10.pdf.

Blyth, Mark, *Austerity: The History of a Dangerous Idea* (Oxford, 2013).

Heilbroner, Robert, *The Worldly Philosophers* (London, 1995).

International Monetary Fund (IMF), 'Reassessing the role and modalities of fiscal policy in advanced economies', IMF policy paper (Washington, DC, 17 Sept. 2013). Online: http://www.imf.org/external/np/pp/eng/2013/072113. pdf.

Jordà, Òscar and Alan M. Taylor, 'The time for austerity: estimating the average treatment effect of fiscal policy', NBER Working Paper No. 19414 (Sept. 2013). Online: http://www.nber.org/papers/w19414.

Krugman, Paul, 'How the case for austerity has crumbled', *New York Review of Books* (6 June 2013). Online: http://www.nybooks.com/articles/archives/2013/jun/06/how-case-austerity-has-crumbled/?pagination=false.

Quiggin, John, *Zombie Economics: How Dead Ideas Still Walk among Us* (Princeton, NJ, 2010).

Schumpeter, Joseph, *History of Economic Analysis* (Oxford, 1994).

Stuckler, David and Sanjay Basu, *The Body Economic: Why Austerity Kills* (New York, 2013).

Wolf, Martin, 'How austerity has failed', *New York Review of Books* (11 July 2013). Online: http://www.nybooks.com/articles/archives/2013/jul/11/how-austerity-has-failed/?pagination=false.

Chapter 1 Austere ideas for austere societies: from Aristotle to Aquinas

Aristotle, *The Nicomachean Ethics* (Oxford, 2009). Online: http://classics.mit.edu.

Aristotle, *The Politics* (London, 1992). Online: http://classics.mit.edu.

Barnes, Jonathan, *Aristotle: A Very Short Introduction* (Oxford, 2000).

The Bible, New Revised Standard Version, Anglicised edn (National Council of the Churches of Christ in the USA, 1995). Online: http://www.oremus.org.

Brown, Lesley, 'Introduction', in Aristotle, *The Nicomachean Ethics* (Oxford, 2009), vii–xxxvii.

Brown, Peter, *Through the Eye of a Needle: Wealth, the Fall of Rome, and the Making of Christianity in the West, 350–550 AD* (Princeton, NJ, 2012).

Fromm, Erich, *To Have or To Be* (New York, 1976).

Kant, Immanuel, *Grounding for the Metaphysics of Morals* (Indianapolis, IN, 1993).

Kerr, Fergus, *Thomas Aquinas: A Very Short Introduction* (Oxford, 2009).

Keynes, John Maynard, *The General Theory of Employment, Interest and Money*, vol. 7 of *The Collected Writings of John Maynard Keynes* (Cambridge, 2013). Online:www.marxists.org

Laertius, Diogenes, *The Lives of the Eminent Philosophers* (2 vols, Cambridge, MA, 1925). Online: http://en.wikisource.org/wiki/Lives_of_the_Eminent_Philosophers.

Loader, James Alfred, *A Tale of Two Cities: Sodom and Gomorrah in the Old Testament, Early Jewish and Early Christian Traditions* (Kampen, NJ, 1990).

Long, Stephen, *Christian Ethics: A Very Short Introduction* (Oxford, 2010).

Morris, Ian et al., eds, *The Cambridge Economic History of the Greco-Roman World* (Cambridge, 2012).

Chapter 2 Austerity v. reason: from Mandeville to Voltaire

Breen, Timothy, *The Marketplace of the Revolution: How Consumer Politics Shaped American Independence* (Oxford, 2004).

Dickie, John, *Delizia. The Epic History of the Italians and their Food* (London, 2007).

Heilbroner, Robert, *Teachings from the Worldly Philosophy* (New York, 1996).

Hirschman, Albert, *The Passions and the Interests: Political Arguments for Capitalism before Its Triumph* (Princeton, NJ, 1997).

Hont, Istvan, 'The early Enlightenment debate on commerce and luxury', in Mark Goldie and Robert Wokler, eds, *The Cambridge History of Eighteenth-Century Political Thought* (Cambridge, 2006), 379–417.

Jones, Colin and Rebecca Spang, 'Sans-culottes, sans café, sans tabac: shifting realms of necessity and luxury in eighteenth-century France', in Maxine Berg and Helen Clifford, eds, *Consumers and Luxury: Consumer Culture in Europe 1650–1850* (Manchester, 1999), 37–62.

Mandeville, Bernard, *The Fable of the Bees or Private Vices, Publick Benefits* (2 vols, Indianapolis, IN, 1988), vol. 1. Online: http://oll.libertyfund.org.

Pomeau, René, *Voltaire en son temps* (2 vols, Oxford, 1995).

Rousseau, Jean-Jacques, *'The Discourses' and Other Early Political Writings* (Cambridge, 1997). Online: http://oll.libertyfund.org.

Rousseau, Jean-Jacques, *'The Social Contract' and Other Later Political Writings* (Cambridge, 1997). Online: http://oll.libertyfund.org.

Schui, Florian, *Rebellious Prussians: Urban Political Culture under Frederick the Great and His Successors* (Oxford, 2013).

Smith, Adam, *An Inquiry into the Wealth of Nations*, ed. Roy Campbell and Andrew Skinner (2 vols, Indianapolis, 1981). Online: http://oll.libertyfund.org.

Voltaire, 'The man of the world', in John Morley, *The Works of Voltaire: A Contemporary Version*, trans. William F. Fleming, annotated Tobias Smollett (21 vols, New York, 1901), vol. 10. Online: http://oll.libertyfund.org.

Voltaire, 'The worldling', in John Morley, *The Works of Voltaire: A Contemporary Version*, trans. William F. Fleming, annotated Tobias Smollett (21 vols, New York, 1901), vol. 10. Online: http://oll.libertyfund.org.

de Vries, Jan, 'The industrial revolution and the industrious revolution', *Journal of Economic History* (1994), 249–70.

Chapter 3 Austerity for capitalism: from Smith to Weber

Banta, Martha, 'Introduction', in Thorstein Veblen, *The Theory of the Leisure Class* (Oxford, 2009).

Cantoni, Davide, 'The economic effects of the Protestant Reformation: testing the Weber hypothesis in the German Lands', working paper (2009). Online: http://www.people.fas.harvard.edu/~cantoni/cantoni_jmp_2_7_1.pdf.

Haakonssen, Knud, ed., *The Cambridge Companion to Adam Smith* (Cambridge, 2006).

Harvey, David, *A Companion to Marx's Capital* (London, 2010).

Heilbroner, Robert and William Milberg, *The Making of Economic Society* (London, 2012).

Käsler, Dirk, *Max Weber: An Introduction to His Life and Work* (Cambridge, 1988).

Keynes, John Maynard, *A Treatise on Money: II, The Applied Theory of Money*, vol. 6 of *The Collected Writings of John Maynard Keynes* (Cambridge, 2013).

Lehmann, Hartmut and Günther Roth, eds, *Weber's Protestant Ethic: Origins, Evidence, Contexts* (Cambridge, 1995).

Marx, Karl, *Capital* (3 vols, Marx/Engels Internet Archive, 2010). Online: www.marxists.org.

Mokyr, Joel, 'Demand vs. supply in the Industrial Revolution', *Journal of Economic History*, 37 (1977), 981–1008.

Morgan, Kenneth, *Slavery, Atlantic Trade and the British Economy, 1660–1800* (Cambridge, 2000).

Smith, Adam, *The Essential Adam Smith*, ed. Robert Heilbroner (New York, 1987).

Smith, Adam, *An Inquiry into the Wealth of Nations*, ed. Roy Campbell and Andrew Skinner (2 vols, Indianapolis, IN, 1981), vol. 1. Online: http://oll.libertyfund.org.

Veblen, Thorstein, *The Theory of the Leisure Class* (Oxford, 2009).

Weber, Max, *The Protestant Ethic and the Spirit of Capitalism and Other Writings* (London, 2002).

Chapter 4 Austerity for stability: from the Great War to the next

Ahamed, Liaquat, *Lords of Finance: The Bankers Who Broke the World* (London, 2009).

Bernstein, Peter, *The Power of Gold: A Story of an Obsession* (New York, 2000).

Borchardt, Knut and Albrecht Ritschl, 'Could Brüning have done it? A Keynesian model of interwar Germany', *European Economic Review*, 37 (1992), 695–701.

Bryan, Steven, *The Gold Standard at the Turn of the Twentieth Century: Rising Powers, Global Money, and the Age of Empire* (New York, 2010).

De Long, J. Bradford, ' "Liquidation cycles": old fashioned real business cycles theory and the Great Depression', NBER Working Paper No. 3546 (1990). Online: http://www.nber.org/papers/w3546.pdf?new_window=1.

Eichengreen, Barry, *Golden Fetters: The Gold Standard and the Great Depression, 1919–1939* (Oxford, 2003).

Eichengreen, Barry and Peter Temin, 'Fetters of gold and paper', *Oxford Review of Economic Policy*, 3 (2010), 370–84.

Eichengreen, Barry and Peter Temin, 'The gold standard and the Great Depression', *Contemporary European History*, 2 (2000), 183–207.

Ford, Alec, 'International financial policy and the gold standard, 1870–1914', in Peter Mathias and Sidney Pollard, eds, *The Cambridge Economic History of Europe*, vol. 8: *The Industrial Economies* (Cambridge, 1989), 197–249.

Herle, J., 'Das Problem der Wirtschaftsdemokratie auf der Düsseldorfer Industrietagung 1929', in *Das Problem der Wirtschaftsdemokratie. Zur Düsseldorfer Tagung des Reichsverbandes der deutschen Industrie* (Düsseldorf, 1929).

Hömig, Herbert, *Brüning: Kanzler in der Krise der Republik* (Paderborn, 2000).

James, Harold, *The German Slump: Politics and Economics, 1924–36* (Oxford, 1986).

James, Robert, *Churchill: A Study in Failure, 1900–1939* (Cleveland, OH, 1970).

Mitchell, B.R., *International Historical Statistics: The Americas 1750–2005* (Basingstoke, 2007).

Mitchell, B.R., *International Historical Statistics: Europe 1750–2005* (Basingstoke, 2007).

Moggridge, Donald, 'The gold standard and national financial policies, 1913–39', in Peter Mathias and Sidney Pollard, eds, *The Cambridge Economic History of Europe*, vol. 8: *The Industrial Economies* (Cambridge, 1989), 250–314.

Schumpeter, Joseph, 'Die Grenzen der Lohnpolitik', *Der Deutsche Volkswirt*, 3 (1928), 847–51, 1022–3.

Weisbrod, Bernd, 'Economic power and political stability reconsidered: heavy industry in Weimar Germany', *Social History*, 4 (1979), 241–263.

Weisbrod, Bernd, *Schwerindustrie in der Weimarer Republik* (Wuppertal, 1978).

Chapter 5 Austerity can wait: Keynes

Burke, Edmund, *Reflections on the Revolution in France* (Oxford, 2009).

Chick, Victoria, 'Economics and the good life: Keynes and Schumacher', paper, World Economics Association conference, 2012. Online: http://weaethics-conference.files.wordpress.com/2012/03/chick-ethics-feb121.pdf.

Daston, Lorraine, *Classical Probability in the Enlightenment* (Princeton, NJ, 1995).

Dorfman, Joseph, *The Economic Mind in American Civilization*, vol. 4 (New York, 1959).

Fenichel, Otto, 'The drive to amass wealth', *Psychoanalytic Quarterly*, 7 (1938), 69–95.

Hayek, Friedrich, 'The "paradox" of saving', *Economica*, 32 (1931), 125–69.

Hayek, Friedrich, 'The road from serfdom', interview with Thomas W. Hazlett, 1977, *Reason Magazine* (July 1992). Online: www.reason.com.

Keynes, John Maynard, 'Economic possibilities for our grandchildren', in Donald Moggridge, ed., *The Collected Writings of John Maynard Keynes*, vol. 9: *Essays in Persuasion* (London, 1972), 321–34. Online: www.marxists.org.

Keynes, John Maynard, 'The general theory of employment', *Quarterly Journal of Economics*, 51 (1937), 209–23.

Keynes, John Maynard, *The General Theory of Employment, Interest and Money*, vol. 7 of *The Collected Writings of John Maynard Keynes* (Cambridge, 2013). Online: www.marxists.org.

Keynes, John Maynard, 'How to avoid a slump', in Donald Moggridge, ed., *The Collected Writings of John Maynard Keynes*, vol. 21: *Activities 1931–1939: World Crises and Policies in Britain and America* (London, 1982), 384–95.

Malthus, Thomas Robert, *The Principles of Political Economy* (London, 1836). Online: http://oll.libertyfund.org.

Nash, Robert and William Gramm, 'A neglected early statement of the paradox of thrift', *History of Political Economy*, 1 (1969), 395–400.

Robinson, Joan, 'The second crisis of economic theory', *American Economic Review*, 62 (1972), 1–10.

Skidelsky, Robert, *John Maynard Keynes: 1883–1946: Economist, Philosopher, Statesman* (London, 2005).

Skidelsky, Robert, *Keynes: The Return of the Master* (London, 2010).

Skidelsky, Robert, *Keynes: A Very Short Introduction* (Oxford, 2010).

Chapter 6 Austerity for the state: Hayek

Ebenstein, Alan, *Friedrich Hayek: A Biography* (New York, 2001).

Friedman, Milton, 'Mr Market' (interview), *Hoover Digest*, 1 (1999). Online: http://www.hoover.org/publications/hoover-digest/article/6459.

Gardner, Howard, *Multiple Intelligences: New Horizons in Theory and Practice* (New York, 2006).

Graham, Andrew and Anthony Seldon, eds, *Government and Economies in the Postwar World: Economic Policies and Comparative Performance 1945–85* (New York, 1990).

Hayek, Friedrich, *The Road to Serfdom* (Chicago, 2007).

Hayek, Friedrich, 'The road from serfdom', interview with Thomas W. Hazlett, 1977, *Reason Magazine* (July 1992). Online: www.reason.com.

Hayek, Friedrich et al., 'Public works from rates', Letter to the editor, *The Times* (of London), 19 Oct. 1932.

Kalecki, Michal, 'Political aspects of full employment', *Political Quarterly* (1943). Online: http://mrzine.monthlyreview.org/2010/kalecki220510.html.

Keynes, John Maynard, *A Tract on Monetary Reform* (Amherst, 2000).

Knight, Frank, 'Reader's report', in Friedrich Hayek, *The Road to Serfdom*, ed. Bruce Caldwell (Chicago, 2007), 249–50.

Middleton, Roger, *Government versus the Market: The Growth of the Public Sector, Economic Management and British Economic Performance, c. 1890–1979* (Cheltenham, 1996).

Offer, Avner, *The Challenge of Affluence: Self-control and Well-being in the United States and Britain since 1950* (Oxford, 2006).

Robinson, Joan, 'The second crisis of economic theory', *American Economic Review*, 62 (1972), 1–10.

Rodgers, Daniel, *Age of Fracture* (Cambridge, MA, 2011).

Scarr, S. 'Developmental theories for the 1990s: development and individual differences', *Child Development*, 63 (1992), 1–19.

Wapshott, Nicholas, *Keynes Hayek: The Clash that Defined Modern Economics* (London, 2011).

Wolf, Martin, 'Thatcher: the great transformer', *Financial Times*, 8 April 2013.

Chapter 7 Austerity for the planet: green ideas of consumption

Attfield, Robin, *The Ethics of Environmental Concern* (Oxford, 1983).

Dobson, Andrew, *Green Political Thought* (London, 2007).

Ehrlich, Paul and Anne Ehrlich, *The End of Affluence: A Blueprint for Your Future* (New York, 1974)

Lomborg, Bjørn, *The Skeptical Environmentalist: Measuring the Real State of the World* (Cambridge, 2012).

Malthus, Thomas, *An Essay on the Principle of Population* (Oxford, 2008). Online: http://oll.libertyfund.org.

Meadows, Donella et al., *The Limits to Growth: A Report for the Club of Rome's Project on the Predicament of Mankind* (London, 1974).

Monbiot, George, *Heat: How We Can Stop the Planet Burning* (London, 2007).

Myers, Norman and Julian Simon, *Scarcity or Abundance? A Debate on the Environment* (New York, 1994).

Randers, Jørgen, *2052: A Global Forecast for the Next Forty Years* (White River Junction, VT, 2012).

Shelley, Mary, *Frankenstein, or The Modern Prometheus* (Oxford, 2008).

Simon, Julian and Herman Kahn, *The Resourceful Earth* (Oxford, 1984).

Chapter 8 Is greed good?

Adorno, Theodor and Max Horkheimer, *Dialectic of Enlightenment* (London, 1997).

Aidt, Toke and Peter Jensen, 'Tax structure, size of government, and the extension of the voting franchise in Western Europe, 1860–1938', Cambridge Working Paper in Economics No. 0715 (2007). Online: http://www.econ.cam.ac.uk/research/repec/cam/pdf/cwpe0715.pdf.

Aidt, Toke, Jayasri Dutta and Elena Loukoianova, 'Democracy comes to Europe: franchise extension and fiscal outcomes 1830–1938', *European Economic Review*, 50 (2006), 249–83.

Edgeworth, Francis Ysidro, *Mathematical Psychics: An Essay on the Application of Mathematics on to the Moral Sciences* (London, 1881).

Fromm, Erich, *To Have or To Be* (New York, 1976).

Galbraith, John Kenneth, *The Affluent Society* (London, 1998).

Gay, Peter, *Voltaire's Politics: The Poet as a Realist* (New York, 1966).

Keynes, John Maynard, 'Economic possibilities for our grandchildren', in Donald Moggridge, ed., *The Collected Writings of John Maynard Keynes*, vol. 9: *Essays in Persuasion* (London, 1972), 321–34. Online: www.marxists.org.

Montesquieu, Charles de Secondat, baron de, *The Spirit of the Laws* (Cambridge, 1989). Online: http://oll.libertyfund.org.

Schumacher, Ernst Friedrich, *Small Is Beautiful: A Study of Economics As If People Mattered* (London, 1993).

Skidelsky, Robert and Edward Skidelsky, *How Much Is Enough? The Love of Money, and the Case for the Good Life* (London, 2012).

Sokoloff, Kenneth and Eric Zolt, 'Inequality and the evolution of institutions of taxation: evidence from the economic history of the Americas', in Sebastian Edwards, Gerardo Esquivel and Graciela Márquez, eds, *The Decline of Latin American Economies: Growth, Institutions, and Crises* (Chicago, 2007), 83–136. Online: http://www.nber.org/chapters/c10654.pdf.

Acknowledgements

While writing this book I have incurred many debts which I would like to acknowledge. First of all, I am grateful to the Leverhulme Trust for generous financial support. Thanks to a Research Fellowship for the project 'The use of historical evidence in public debates about fiscal crises since 1750' I was relieved of teaching duties and could focus on research and writing. I am also grateful to the Department of History at Royal Holloway for granting me additional leave and allowing me to take up the fellowship.

I would also like to thank colleagues and students in the department. Scholarly discussions and informal conversations with colleagues at Royal Holloway have contributed much to this book and have made the department a pleasant and inspiring place to work. Some of the ideas that found their way into this book I have 'tried out' on students who took my course 'The lever of riches: perspectives on capitalism' in the last years. I would like to thank them for lively discussions and the many good questions which they asked.

As the manuscript began to take shape I benefited enormously from the comments of those who read it in part or in its entirety. I thank in particular David Gwynn, Rudolf Muhs,

Adam Larragy, Gemma Simmonds CJ, Herbert Schui, Malte Woweries and several anonymous readers. I am equally indebted to those who have commented on this project at seminars to which I have been invited. I also wish to thank Heather McCallum and everyone at Yale University Press for supporting this project and for being extremely efficient and helpful.

Without good libraries and the support of many librarians this book would not have been possible. I would therefore like to thank the staff at the British Library, Biblioteca Nazionale Braidense and Biblioteca di Scienze della Storia e della Documentazione Storica at Università degli Studi di Milano.

Index